D1279128

THE INDUSTRIAL REVOLUTION: SOCIAL AND ECONOMIC EFFECTS

LUCENT LIBRARY of HISTORICAL ERAS

THE INDUSTRIAL REVOLUTION: SOCIAL AND ECONOMIC EFFECTS

DON NARDO

LUCENT BOOKS
A part of Gale, Cengage Learning

GALE
CENGAGE Learning™

Detroit • New York • San Francisco • New Haven, Conn • Waterville, Maine • London

LIBRARY OF CONGRESS CATALOGING-IN-PUBLICATION DATA

Nardo, Don, 1947-
  Industrial Revolution : social and economic effects / by Don Nardo.
    p. cm. — (The Lucent library of historical eras)
  Includes bibliographical references and index.
  ISBN 978-1-4205-0151-3 (hardcover)
  1. Industrial revolution. 2. Economic history. I. Title.
  HD2321.N37 2009
  330.9'034—dc22
                                        2008053576

Lucent Books
27500 Drake Rd.
Farmington Hills, MI 48331

ISBN-13: 978-1-4205-0151-3
ISBN-10: 1-4205-0151-8

Printed in the United States of America
1 2 3 4 5 6 7 13 12 11 10 09

Contents

Foreword

Looking back from the vantage point of the present, history can be viewed as a myriad of intertwining roads paved by human events. Some paths stand out—broad highways whose mileposts, even from a distance of centuries, are clear. The events that propelled the rise to power of Germany's Third Reich, its role in World War II, and its eventual demise, for example, are well defined and documented.

Other roads are less distinct, their route sometimes hidden from view. Modern legislatures may have developed from old tribal councils, for example, but the links between them are indistinct in places, open to discussion and interpretation.

The architecture of civilization—law, religion, art, science, and government—as well as the more everyday aspects of our culture—what we eat, what we wear—all developed along the historical roads and byways. In that progression can be traced every facet of modern life.

A broad look back along these roads reveals that many paths—though of vastly different character—seem to converge at a few critical junctions. These intersections are those great historical eras that echo over the long, steady course of human history, extending beyond the past and into the present.

These epic periods of time are the focus of Historical Eras. They shine through the mists of history like beacons, illuminated by a burst of creativity that propels events forward—so bright that we, from thousands of years away, can clearly see the chain of events leading to the present.

Each Historical Eras consists of a set of books that highlight various aspects of these major eras. For example, the Elizabethan England library features volumes on Queen Elizabeth I and her court, Elizabethan theater, the great playwrights, and everyday life in Elizabethan London.

The mini-library approach allows for the division of each era into its most significant and most interesting parts and the exploration of those parts in depth. Also, social and cultural trends as well as illustrative documents and eyewitness accounts can be prominently featured in individual volumes.

Historical Eras presents a wealth of information to young readers. The lively narrative, fully documented primary and secondary source quotations, maps, photographs, sidebars, and annotated bibliographies serve as launching points for class discussion and further research.

In studying the great historical eras, students also develop a better understanding of our own times. What we learn from the past and how we apply it in the present may shape the future and may determine whether our era will be a guiding light to those traveling future roads.

Introduction

ON THE VERGE OF A GREAT MOVEMENT

The technical and economic effects of the Industrial Revolution in Britain and the United States were fairly plain to see as this historical event unfolded. Machines were doing many of the routine jobs that had long been done by hand. Steam-driven and eventually electrically powered looms replaced hand-operated ones, for instance. Factories churned out all manner of consumer goods. And natural resources such as coal and oil were harnessed to provide energy on a vast scale, while industry created new, faster forms of transportation, including trains and automobiles. At the same time, noted scholar Laura L. Frader points out, "the industrial centers, towns, and cities that sprang up around [the factories] were linked by an increasingly efficient system of roads, rivers and canals, and rail-

ways."[1] These and other factors generated enormous economic expansion and made Britain and the United States major industrial and economic powers.

How and to what degree large-scale industrialization was altering society was less obvious. Political and social leaders and writers of the nineteenth and early twentieth centuries wondered how social customs and attitudes might change and if moral values would change as well.

Benefits to Society

Some of these individuals were optimistic about the ongoing changes and about the future these changes would bring. The noted nineteenth-century American historian and thinker William Graham Sumner, for instance, saw large-scale industry as a positive guiding force for society. The overall standard of living had risen in the industrial age, he said. And it was only natural that people's lives would adjust to the new conditions created. Sumner wrote in 1894 that industrialization

> creates the conditions of our existence, sets the limits of our social activity, regulates the bonds of our social relations, determines our conceptions of good and evil, suggests our life-philosophy, molds our inherited political institutions, and reforms the oldest and toughest customs, like marriage and property. [All of this] gives us great social power. It is to [industrialization] that we owe our increased comfort and abundance. We are none of us ready to sacrifice this. On the contrary, we want more of it. We would not return to the colonial simplicity [of the 1700s] if we could.[2]

This editorial cartoon shows laborers struggling to hold up and protect such millionaires as Jay Gould and Cornelius Vanderbilt. Business tycoons like these typically underpaid and mistreated their employees.

The Downsides of Industrialization

In contrast, economic historian Matthew Josephson was more critical of industry's effects on society. In his influential 1934 book, *The Robber Barons*, he criticized a number of the big industrialists of the late 1800s and early 1900s. They were "aggressive men" and "feudal barons," he asserted. They amassed immense wealth by exploiting laborers, who worked long, hard days and still could barely make ends meet. "Sometimes they were lawless," Josephson said about John D. Rockefeller, Jay Gould, Cornelius Vanderbilt, and other successful business tycoons. Josephson continued:

> In important crises, nearly all of them tended to act without those established moral principles which [guided] . . . the conduct of the common people of the community. . . . To organize and exploit the resources of a nation upon a gigantic scale, to regiment its farmers and workers into harmonious corps of producers, and to do this only in the name of an uncontrolled appetite for private profit —here surely is the [source of] so much disaster, outrage and misery.[3]

Josephson's use of the words *disaster* and *misery* referred to what he and other critics saw as serious downsides of the Industrial Revolution. Industrialization had caused or intensified poverty in many regions, they pointed out. Also,

they claimed, the cruel child labor practices and unhealthy working conditions typical in early factories were not positive changes. In addition, there was much polluted air and water and other environmental destruction as a result of industrialization.

American political economist and philosopher Henry George was also critical of certain aspects of rapid and widespread industrialization. He saw the potential inequalities, injustices, and other negative effects that might result from a few wealthy, privileged individuals, like Rockefeller and Vanderbilt, controlling society. But he was not ready to condemn industry itself, which he conceded might bring some measure of good. "What change may come, no mortal man can tell," George wrote in his classic book *Progress and Poverty*, published in 1883. "But that some great change must come, thoughtful men begin to feel. The civilized world is trembling on the verge of a great movement. Either it must be a leap upward, which will open the way to advances yet undreamed of, or it must be a plunge downward, which will carry us back toward barbarism."[4]

Society's Compromise

Much has happened since George composed these words. And today most people, historians and nonhistorians alike, would agree that neither the optimists nor pessimists of his era got it completely right. Rather, history has shown that in-

There were many positive effects of the Industrial Revolution, including the mechanization of agriculture, which increased food production and facilitated population growth.

dustry and technology have had both positive and negative effects on society.

Among the negative effects, environmental destruction caused by industry continued in many areas throughout the twentieth century. Entire forests disappeared. Hundreds of rivers and lakes were polluted, in some cases so badly that all the fish in them died. And giant oil tankers foundered, ruining miles of coastline and killing millions of birds. Noted American conservationist John Burroughs lamented: "A nature fertile and bountiful . . . has been outraged and disfigured and impoverished."[5]

State and federal governments were eventually forced to enact environmental protection laws. But some were not

Folly to Resist the Stream of Time?

Nineteenth-century American thinker William Graham Sumner argued that the ongoing Industrial Revolution was not something that people could control. Rather, industrialization and the social changes it created inevitably controlled society and sent it in new, sometimes unpredictable directions. "The great stream of time and earthly things will sweep on just the same in spite of us," he stated in a powerful 1894 essay.

Every one of us is a child of his age and cannot get out of it. He is in the stream and is swept along with it. All of his sciences and philosophy come to him out of it. Therefore the tide will not be changed by us. It will swallow up both us and our experiments. . . . The things which will change it are the great discoveries and inventions, [and] the new reactions inside the social organism. . . . [It is a] vain fantasy that we can make or guide the [industrial and technological] movement. That is why it is the greatest folly . . . to sit down with a slate and pencil to plan out a new social world.

Quoted in A.G. Keller and M.R. Davie, eds., *Essays of William Graham Sumner.* New Haven, CT: Yale University Press, 1940, p. 97.

rigidly enforced at first. Moreover, evidence is now overwhelming that human output of carbon dioxide and other greenhouse gases, most of them produced by industry, are causing potentially dangerous climate changes on a global scale.

On the positive side, it is clear that many changes wrought by the rise of industry and technology have been good for society. The mechanization of agriculture allowed for the production of more food, making it possible to sustain much larger populations. More advanced forms of transportation made travel faster, easier, and less expensive.

And the telegraph, telephone, radio, television, and computer, all products of the Industrial Revolution, made communications faster and information more accessible. Furthermore, hundreds of millions of people were spared pain and death thanks to advances in medicine made possible by industrialization and the many new technologies it generated.

It cannot be denied that Sumner was right when he said that few are ready to give up these accumulated fruits of progress. Returning to a simpler past in which all products were made by hand, cross-country travel took months, and millions died of diseases now easily treatable is out of the question. As Sumner himself pointed out, society learned to compromise between the good and bad effects of the industrial age. "We must pay the price" for the benefits that industrialization has brought, he said.

"Our life is bounded on every side by conditions. We can have this if we will agree to submit to that."[6] It may well be that, barring any major events no one can now foresee, this societal compromise will remain in effect for a long time to come.

Chapter One

RESISTANCE TO A CHANGING WORLD

When factories began to sprout up across Britain and the United States in the early decades of the industrial age, attitudes toward them were divided. On the one hand, owners, who came to be called industrialists, were optimistic. They were eager to build more factories and fill them with the power looms and other machines that were rapidly transforming manufacturing processes. This attitude was understandable. After all, well-to-do businessmen who could afford to build factories stood to make a great deal of money from industrialization.

On the other hand, many people who had long made yarn, clothes, and other products by hand in their homes could not compete with the factories. Large numbers of them lost their livelihoods in the late 1700s and early 1800s. In desperation, some took jobs in the very places that had put them out of work—the factories. Of these workers, some were simply grateful to have some way of making a living. But many others found new grievances, including long hours, low pay, little or no job security, and unhealthy or unsafe working conditions.

Not surprisingly, many people who found themselves in these unhappy situations protested in one way or another. In retrospect, these protests can be seen as part of widespread resistance to change that swept through British and American societies in the early years of the Industrial Revolution.

Sources of Anger and Unrest

The frustrations and discontent many workers felt during the early years of industrialization were rooted in their anxiety about the social changes machines were causing. As Laura L. Frader says,

"Many men and women feared that new technologies, the hallmark of the Industrial Revolution, promised not progress and prosperity, but a loss of skill, status, wages, and employment."[7] In the words of two chroniclers of the Industrial Revolution, James Outman and Elizabeth Outman, the workers "complained that because the machines could produce so much more yarn or wool in a day, many people who formerly worked at home could no longer find work. They asked what would happen to them and their families if newer machines kept being introduced, causing more jobs to disappear."[8]

This fear of losing jobs proved well grounded. In the county of Yorkshire in northeast England, for example, there were about five thousand villagers and farmers engaged in making wool in 1806. Some sheared the sheep, others combed and cleaned the wool, and still others turned it into yarn on hand-operated spindles. It was a home-centered manufacturing system that had existed for centuries.

This cottage wool industry was doomed to disappear in less than a generation, however. By 1812 six or seven water-powered factories existed in Yorkshire. A man named William Cartwright

A man works in a wool mill near Leeds, Yorkshire, England.

had a small wool factory in Yorkshire that featured fifty wool-finishing machines powered by a waterwheel set in the stream running beside the structure. Each of Cartwright's machines did the work of five or six home-centered wool workers. So those workers could not compete with the new factories. By 1817 only about 760 people in Yorkshire still made wool by hand. And by 1830, fewer than a hundred did so.

This dramatic loss of jobs was not the only thing that caused anger and unrest in the countryside. Traditional workers were also upset over the new economic philosophy taking hold in the country, one in which politics played an increasing role. "Those who controlled capital [big money]," scholar Kirkpatrick Sale writes, "were able to do almost anything they wished, encouraged and protected by government and king, without much in the way of laws or ethics or customs to restrain them."[9] This became a sort of moral challenge to many of the workers. They called into question the fairness and justice of a system in which new machines and ideas threatened to destroy their traditional lifestyle, which they viewed as stable, honest, and beneficial.

Peaceful Protests Attempted

Moved by such concerns, in 1786 cloth makers in Leeds (in northern England) protested. They wrote a petition to the wealthy merchants who had recently opened cloth-making factories in Leeds. It stated in part:

[The new] machines have thrown thousands of your petitioners out of employ[ment], whereby they are brought into great distress, and are not able to procure a maintenance [earn a living] for their families. . . . Each machine will do as much work in twelve hours as ten men can in that time do by hand. . . . How are those men, thus thrown out of employ[ment], to provide for their families? [And] what are their children to do? Are they to be brought up in idleness?[10]

The petition concluded with a call for the factory owners to be reasonable and acquire no more machines. But this and other early protests against the new industry fell on deaf ears. The merchants and factory owners countered that machines increased profits, made the country more competitive and thereby stronger, and were part of progress.

The Luddites Versus the "Frames"

Unable to stop the onrush of the machine age by peaceful protests, some English laborers resorted to violence. These individuals attacked factories and destroyed the machines, which were then commonly called frames. Such machine breakers became known as Luddites. The Outmans explain the derivation of the term:

The vandals sent letters signed with the name "General Ned Ludd" (or

A nineteenth-century illustration shows the Luddites rioting in protest of the increase in the mechanization of jobs.

variations of this name, such as Ned Ludd or Edward Ludd). Some historians think Ned Ludd was the name of an actual person, a man of limited intelligence who lived in the area of Leicestershire, England, around 1779. ...Other historians say that Ned Ludd was a ... fictitious character, a pseudonym (false name) used to disguise the identity of the letter writers.[11]

Regardless of whether Ned Ludd himself was real, the raw emotions of those who called him their leader were quite real. They usually claimed to be driven to violence out of feelings of outrage and desperation. In an awkwardly written letter penned in 1802, one Luddite admitted that wrecking machines was ethically wrong but that he had been driven to it:

The burning of Factorys or setting fire to the property of People we know is not right, but Starvation forces Nature to do that which he would not, nor would it reach his Thoughts had he sufficient Employ[ment]. We have tried every Effort to live by Pawning our Cloaths and Chattles [belongings], so we are now on the brink for the last struggle.[12]

The Luddites' resentment and anger is also plain to see in the warning letters they routinely sent to factory owners before the attacks. The owner of a Yorkshire textile mill received this ominous message in 1812:

Information has just been given [that] you are a holder of those detestable shearing frames [textile machines], and I was desired by my men to write to you, and give you fair warning to pull them down. . . . If they are not taken down by the end of next week, I shall [send] at least 300 men to destroy them [and] we will increase your misfortunes by burning your buildings down to ashes, and if you have the impudence to fire at any of my men, they have orders to murder you. . . . Signed by the General of the Army of Redressers. Ned Ludd.[13]

The mischief the Luddites threatened was reflected as well in the patriotic songs they created, including the following:

And night by night when all is still
And the moon is hid behind the hill,

A Secret Luddite Oath

The Luddites often demanded that new recruits to their organization swear some sort of oath. Of those that survive, one states:

I [the recruit's name] of my own voluntary will, do declare, and solemnly swear, that I never will reveal to any person or persons under the canopy of heaven, the names of the persons who compose this Secret Committee, their proceedings, meeting [places], places of abode, dress, features, connections, or anything else that might lead to a discovery of the same, either by word or deed. . . . I further now do swear that I will use my best endeavors to punish by death any traitor or traitors, should any rise up against us. . . . I will pursue him with increasing vengeance. So help me God.

Quoted in Kirkpatrick Sale, *Rebels Against the Future: The Luddites and Their War on the Industrial Revolution.* Cambridge, MA: Perseus, 1996, pp. 107–108.

We forward march to do our will
With hatchet, pike, and gun!
Oh, the cropper [farmer] lads for
  me,
The gallant lads for me,
Who with lusty stroke
The shear frames broke,
The cropper lads for me![14]

Groups of angry Luddites put such aggressive words into practice on many occasions in the early years of the nineteenth century. A local newspaper, the *Annual Register*, described an assault on the cloth factory of a well-to-do Yorkshire merchant named Joseph Foster in April 1812: "A large body of armed men . . . completely destroyed all the shears and frames. . . . They then demolished all the windows, and, as if [driven] by the most diabolical [devilish] frenzy, broke into the . . . weaving shops and materially injured the machinery, and wantonly destroyed a quantity of [cloth] ready for the loom."[15]

Though bold and sometimes frightening, the threat of Luddism was relatively short lived. By 1820 there were no more organized attacks of any consequence on factories and machines in Britain. The reasons for this are somewhat unclear. But it is likely that the government's tough crackdown on what Sale calls the "rebels against the future" had much to do with it. Fifteen Luddites were killed in the act of vandalism, twenty-four were captured and hung, thirty-seven were shipped to a penal colony in Australia, and two dozen more

went to prison. Perhaps because Luddism failed and quickly faded in Britain, it never took root in America, where large-scale industry was slower in getting started.

Strikes and Other Protests

In their heyday, the Luddites and their violent antics dominated the headlines in Britain. Less extreme and news grabbing were other forms of workers' protests that occurred both before and after those of the machine breakers. These other protesters were not home workers trying to stop industrialization, but rather employees of the factories. Hoping to obtain shorter hours, higher wages, and better working conditions, they staged strikes.

Such strikes were particularly frequent in the textile industry. Cotton spinners in Lancashire, in northwestern England, struck in 1799, 1800, 1802, 1803, 1810, and 1818, for instance. Some dissatisfied workers formed groups that met to formulate and voice their grievances and demands. A mixed meeting of male and female textile workers in the Lancashire town of Blackburn in July 1818 called for higher wages to alleviate growing poverty in their ranks:

The industrious laborer ought to have a far greater quantity of produce [food and other basic goods] than he [has now]. Instead of which, by means of taxation and restrictive laws, he is reduced to wretchedness [poverty]. Thousands of our countrymen [are starving] in the midst of plenty. No man can have a right to enjoy another man's labor without his consent.[16]

Many strikes were staged in the early years of the U.S. textile industry as well. Women workers in Pawtucket, Rhode Island, struck in 1824, for example. One of the biggest and most famous labor walkouts occurred in 1836 in the mill town of Lowell, Massachusetts. Upset over a proposed pay cut, nearly two thousand women struck, forcing several mills to shut down. One of the leading strikers, Harriet H. Robinson, later remembered: "As I looked back at the long line [of young women] that followed me, I was more proud than I have ever been since at any success I may have achieved, and more proud than I shall ever be again until my own beloved State gives to its women citizens the right of suffrage [voting]."[17]

Mill strikes were frequent in the textile industry during the early to mid-nineteenth century.

An Early Workers' Protest Song

Among the early protestors in the Industrial Revolution were women workers in the textile mills of Massachusetts and Rhode Island. Unhappy with their working conditions, some went on strike in the 1830s. And while marching up and down in front of their factories, they frequently sang songs like this one:

Oh, isn't it a pity, such a pretty girl as I—

Should be sent into the factory to pine away and die?

Oh I cannot be a slave,

I will not be a slave,

For I'm so fond of liberty,

That I cannot be a slave.

Quoted in Laura L. Frader, *The Industrial Revolution: A History in Documents.* New York: Oxford University Press, 2006, p. 113.

Unfortunately for Robinson and her fellow workers, their bosses were not moved and enacted the pay cut in spite of the strike. In fact, most of the early laborers' strikes in Britain, the United States, and other industrialized countries were unsuccessful. One reason was that employers of that era had a great deal of power over their workers. They could not only fire them, but also in many cases evict them from their homes, since mill owners frequently owned the workers' housing, too. Also, the governments of these nations were highly supportive of big business. Frader points out:

On both sides of the Atlantic, governments supported employers' efforts to repress labor organization. France, Britain, and Germany all made workers' organizations of any kind illegal until the end of the nineteenth century. In the United States and Europe, employers combated unions by firing or locking workers out of the factory and freely used police force to repress workers' peaceful demonstrations.[18]

Cooperatives Against Industry

Still another early form of resistance to and protest against the factory system was for workers to withdraw voluntarily from the traditional workforce. As an alternative, they created workers' (or producers') cooperatives. These were, in a sense, self-contained little communities in which the members grew food and made clothes and other products for the greater good. In 1822 the editor of a London newspaper, the *Economist,* called for his readers to join such a cooperative, saying:

> [A] new and grand cooperation, affording ample security for your comfortable and abundant subsistence [has formed]. . . . The families contribute to a common fund for providing for the necessaries of life, at wholesale prices. . . . The families breakfast, dine, etc. together at the general tables, and in the evenings amuse themselves with conversation, reading, lectures, music, etc. . . . The domestic duties of the females are performed [in a cooperative manner], which greatly lessens their labor. . . .

The society already employs its own shoemakers and tailors, and will speedily be enabled to perform all its own work within itself.[19]

Progress Marches Onward

Neither the machine breakers nor the strikers nor the cooperatives made any significant dent in the Industrial Revolution, however. The age of machines sped onward and upward, absorbing or burying nearly all resistance to the societal changes it was bringing about. Big companies got even bigger. And an increasingly large proportion of the population came to work for the owners of these companies, whose social influence often matched their business clout.

Chapter Two

THE "ROBBER BARONS" AND THE GILDED AGE

Among the hallmarks and enduring symbols of the Industrial Revolution were factories, the steam locomotive, the internal combustion engine, and the assembly line. No less important and memorable than these inventions were a small group of remarkable individuals who used them to accumulate immense fortunes and build financial and social empires during the late 1800s and early 1900s. Their ranks included such famous men (or *infamous* ones, depending on one's point of view) as Cornelius Vanderbilt, John D. Rockefeller, Jay Gould, J.P. Morgan, and Andrew Carnegie.

Collectively, they were and remain best known as the robber barons. This unflattering term was coined by historians and others of that era who saw these wealthy individuals as greedy and dishonest. According to one modern expert,

in this less than admirable image they were "predators who grew rich through tactics that were unethical at best, illegal at worst, and contrary to the public interest in any case. They bilked companies, corrupted public officials, and defrauded rivals in their quest for gain."[20]

In the interest of fairness and historical accuracy, however, in recent years a number of historians have sought to modify this unfavorable portrait. Scholars still generally agree that Vanderbilt and most of the others were extremely ambitious and sometimes downright ruthless. Yet as historian Maury Klein points out, they also displayed many distinctly positive traits and talents. "They were masters of organization—visionaries and risk takers who thought and acted on a grand scale," he says. Many of them also used their great wealth to support the arts, education, and social causes. Klein adds that these men made their fortunes during a period of unique and unprecedented economic opportunity:

In the years following the Civil War, land, resources, and cheap labor abounded, while the political and legal system offered fewer restraints to individual action than existed anywhere else on the globe. Never before—or (arguably) since—have opportunities been so ripe for those capable of mobilizing capital and organizing large enterprises. The entrepreneurs who came to dominate this scramble were to the American economy what the Founding Fathers were to the political system.[21]

Klein uses the word *entrepreneurs* (enterprising businesspersons) in place of *robber barons*. Other less judgmental terms for the financial giants of the Industrial Revolution include *industrialists*, *capitalists*, and *captains of industry*. Whatever one chooses to call them, they and their companies were key factors in the industrialization process. They transformed business practices, especially in the United States, and in many ways created the capitalist system that exists today. They also transformed society by creating new kinds of products and jobs, building housing for workers, and ushering in what came to be called the Gilded Age. This consisted of mansion building and other extravagant displays of the wealth these men had amassed.

Choking Out the Competition

Before examining how the great industrialists altered society, one must understand how they changed the way business was conducted. Competition had been part of the bedrock of the market system used in Europe and America for several centuries.

Railroad tycoon Cornelius Vanderbilt built much of his empire by using unscrupulous business techniques.

A person or company that could build a better product or provide a more effective service had an edge on competitors. And this could and often did lead to success.

However, men like Cornelius Vanderbilt (1794–1877) took this philosophy to a new level by seeking an increasingly bigger edge on their competitors. They often did so by employing business practices that others viewed as disreputable, or at the least harsh and cold blooded. Vanderbilt began as a successful owner of steam ferries and freighters in the American Northeast. One way that he learned to increase his profits was to scrimp on safety equipment, including lifeboats and life jackets, for his boats. He also engaged in rate-cutting tactics that drove many of his competitors out of business. In the 1840s, for instance, he became involved in a fare war with his chief rival, the Hudson River Steamboat Association. Vanderbilt started offering free fares to customers. Unable to compete, the other company suffered huge losses and paid Vanderbilt a large sum simply to keep his ships off the Hudson for a few years.

"The Commodore," as Vanderbilt came to be known, later employed similar practices to build a railroad empire. These included buying up stock in many different railroad companies until he had enough power to force several of them to merge. This gave him a monopoly (exclusive control over an industry or service). When one person or company enjoys a monopoly, competition is usually stifled and the person with the monopoly wields enormous power in both the financial and social worlds. Increasingly, people in high places came to think of such monopolies not only as a reality of life, but also as a fitting, beneficial one. An influential Supreme Court judge stated in 1893: "It is the unvarying [natural] law that the wealth of the community will be in the hands of the few . . . and hence it has always been, and until human nature is remodeled always will be true, that the wealth of a nation is in the hands of a few, while the many subsist upon the proceeds of their daily toil."[22]

Strongly adhering to this belief, other industrialists created huge monopolies, including the oil tycoon John D. Rockefeller (1839–1937). Beginning in the 1860s, with ruthless efficiency he bought or drove out of business most of the competing American oil refineries. The discouraged director of one of these companies remarked: "If we did not sell out [we] would be crushed out. . . . There was only one buyer on the market and we had to sell at their terms. [I] felt as if, rather than fight with such a monopoly, I would withdraw from the business."[23] By 1877 Rockefeller controlled 90 percent of all the oil refineries in the country. In this way, he and a few other largely unregulated, unrestrained industrialists came to dominate the workings of the U.S. economy.

These powerful individuals also loomed large in the social circles of the rich, famous, and well connected. Bankers, politicians, and government officials often catered to and received favors from the

Oil tycoon John D. Rockefeller built a huge monopoly to dominate his industry.

dustries were the first beneficiaries of the "welfare state" [in which the government financially supports an individual or organization]. By the turn of the century, American Telephone and Telegraph had a monopoly of the nation's telephone system, International Harvester made 85 percent of all farm machinery, and in every other industry resources became concentrated, controlled. The banks had interests in so many of these monopolies as to create an interlocking network of powerful corporation directors, each of whom sat on the boards of many other corporations. . . . [J.P.] Morgan at his peak sat on the board of forty-eight corporations.[24]

leading entrepreneurs, making all involved a bit wealthier and more successful. Noted historian Howard Zinn writes that many industries were shaped by

> shrewd, efficient businessmen building empires, choking out competition, maintaining high prices, keeping wages low, using government subsidies. These in-

Business Owners Directly Influence Workers' Lives

In addition to hobnobbing with society's elite, the entrepreneurs who accumulated great wealth directly affected, and sometimes even controlled, the lives of people in lower social circles, classes, and towns. One way was through the employer-employee relationship. Each industrialist had thousands, in some cases tens of thousands, of workers who were dependent on him for their livelihoods. If a company owner expanded his business empire, he usually hired more workers, which brought prosperity to both individuals and the towns they lived in. Conversely, industrialists sometimes laid off some of their workers and caused families and towns to suffer.

Some captains of industry controlled their workers in a more direct way. One of the major social developments of the initial decades of the Industrial Revolution was factory owners' creation of housing for workers near their factories. This approach was pioneered by Frances Cabot Lowell (1775–1817) and other leading figures of the early textile industry. In 1822 Lowell and his partners began building mills in a small town about 30 miles (48 km) north of Boston. (The village grew into the city of Lowell, named for him.) By 1834 Lowell had nineteen mills that together employed thousands of people. Most were young women who required a place to live, and

he addressed that need by building boardinghouses. According to modern historians, in Lowell the residents' lives outside of work

came under the watchful eye of boardinghouse keepers, who were required to report any misconduct to mill management. Typically 30 to 40 young women lived together in a boardinghouse. The first floor usually contained a kitchen, dining room, and the keeper's quarters. Upstairs bedrooms accommodated four to eight women, commonly sleeping two in a double bed. In these close quarters, experienced workers helped new hands adapt to their situation.[25]

Clearly, any workers who did not follow the rules at work or who took part

Praise for Industry's "Captains"

In 1894 prominent American historian and thinker William Graham Sumner, who was pro-industry, defined the so-called captains of industry this way:

[T]he ongoing Industrial Revolution] has brought about a great demand for men capable of managing great enterprises. Such have been called "captains of

industry." The analogy with military leaders . . . is not misleading. The great [industrial] leaders [require] those talents of executive and administrative skill, power of command, courage, and fortitude, which were formerly called for in military affairs.

Quoted in A.G. Keller and M.R. Davie, eds., *Essays of William Graham Sumner.* New Haven, CT: Yale University Press, 1940, p. 94.

Smokestacks from textile mills dominate the skyline of Lowell, Massachusetts.

in strikes put themselves in danger of losing their housing as well as their jobs.

Industrialization and the Middle Class

As time went on, the big industrialists and their companies impacted society in more extensive and positive ways. In particular, as these companies grew they indirectly contributed to the growth of the nation's middle class. This happened partly because of the kinds of people the companies hired and trained. In order to become and remain profitable, these large companies needed a certain num-

ber of skilled, loyal middle managers in addition to ordinary factory workers and laborers. One modern observer explains:

With their vastly increased output and costs, firms had to make sure their products sold. Employment multiplied, as firms added new departments such as purchasing, advertising, and sales divisions to supplement their multi-plant manufacturing operations. [And] they had to adopt new, more rational corporate structures. Middle managers multiplied as firms needed larger numbers of specialists to handle the new functions and coordinate the activities of truly giant enterprises.[26]

Typically, these men (women were not considered for managerial positions at the time) started working for a company in a lesser capacity when they were about twenty. After a series of promotions, by age forty or so they had risen to well-paying jobs such as station manager or

The Rich Deserve to Be Rich?

One of the social consequences of the huge fortunes that were amassed and spent during the so-called Gilded Age was an increase in the desire to get rich among people in all social classes. One of the biggest promoters of this idea was a former Protestant preacher named Russell Conwell. For years he traveled around the country giving a speech titled "Acres of Diamonds," excerpted here. His main thesis was that the rich are rich because they deserve it, while the poor are poor because they are sinners.

I say that you ought to get rich, and it is your duty to get rich. . . . "Oh," but says some young man here to-night, "I have been told all my life that if a person has money he is very dishonest and dishonorable." . . . Let me say here clearly . . . ninety-eight out of one hundred of the rich men of America are honest. That is why they are rich. That is why they are trusted with money. . . . Some men say, "Don't you sympathize with the poor

people?" Of course I do. [But] the number of poor who are to be sympathized with is very small. To sympathize with a man whom God has punished for his sins . . . is to do wrong. [There] is not a poor person in the United States who was not made poor by his own shortcomings or the shortcomings of someone else.

Quoted in History Matters, "Russell Conwell Explains Why Diamonds Are a Man's Best Friend." http://history matters.gmu.edu/d/5769.

Russell Conwell promoted the idea that the rich are rich because they deserve it.

train engineer or conductor. These individuals and others who received promotions were able to support families and live middle-class lifestyles; this included sending their children to decent schools so that later they, too, could find well-paying jobs. In fact, wages for large numbers of Americans doubled between 1870 and 1900.

How to Spend a Fortune?

Thus, many Americans, especially in the middle class, were financially better off in the thriving economy created by the great industrialists. Yet the lifestyles and social opportunities of even the best-paid workers did not remotely compare with those of the industrialists themselves. Vanderbilt, Rockefeller, and others in that elite group made fortunes of hundreds of millions of dollars in an age when an average middle-class worker made less than a thousand dollars a year. (The sum of $100 million in 1880 equates to many billions of dollars in today's money.)

The question for these financial giants was what to do with all that money. Most chose to spend it in one of three ways. Some of the money went back into the companies to update equipment, build new factories, and so forth. Considerably more of the money, however, went toward supporting lavish lifestyles for the factory owners and their families. The period from about 1870 to 1893, when these captains of industry were at their height of power, became known as the Gilded Age. (To gild something is to cover it in gold.) It was characterized by outward displays of wealth that most ordinary people viewed as excessive, self-indulgent, and even obscene.

Perhaps the most visible and famous of these displays were the giant mansions erected by the great industrialists and their family members. They remain potent symbols of the enormous wealth produced by and during the industrial age. Among the most splendid of all were those built by the Vanderbilts in the late 1800s and early 1900s. The founder of the family fortune, Cornelius Vanderbilt, preferred to live in fairly modest residences. But his offspring used large portions of the Vanderbilt fortune to create estates and homes of amazing size and beauty. Cornelius's grandson, George W. Vanderbilt II, for example, built Biltmore House in Asheville, North Carolina, in the early 1890s. Having an interior space of 175,000 square feet (16,258 sq. m)—divided into 250 rooms, including 43 bathrooms—it remains the largest private residence in the United States.

The third way that many of the great industrialists spent their vast fortunes was philanthropy (giving money to worthy causes). Even some of the more ruthless of these individuals felt a duty to give back some of the wealth they had accumulated to society. John D. Rockefeller, for instance, gave 10 percent of all his earnings to his church even while building his fortune. Later, he championed American education. He founded Spelman College in Atlanta for young

One example of industrialists using their great wealth in a self-indulgent manner is Biltmore House in Asheville, North Carolina, built by Cornelius Vanderbilt's grandson, George, in the early 1890s.

The "Robber Barons" and the Gilded Age   31

Is Inheriting Industrial Wealth Good for Society?

American industrialist Andrew Carnegie felt that wealthy people had a duty to share their riches with society. In his 1889 essay, "The Gospel of Wealth," he criticized the idea of rich individuals leaving most or all of their wealth to their offspring, who, he held, so often wasted it.

Why should men leave great fortunes to their children? If this is done from affection, is it not misguided affection? Observation teaches that, generally speaking, it is not well for the children that they should be so burdened. Neither is it well for the state. . . . There are instances of millionaires' sons unspoiled by wealth, who, being rich, still perform great services in the community. Such are the very salt of the earth, as valuable as, unfortunately, they are rare; still it is not the exception, but the rule, that men must regard, and, looking at the usual result of enormous sums conferred upon legatees, the thoughtful man must shortly say, "I would as soon leave to my son a curse as the almighty dollar," and admit to himself that it is not the welfare of the children, but family pride, which inspires these enormous legacies.

Andrew Carnegie, "Carnegie, Gospel of Wealth," Swarthmore College. www.swarthmore.edu/SocSci/rbannis1/AIH19th/Carnegie.html.

Andrew Carnegie believed that the wealthy should share their good fortune with the rest of society.

African American women; gave $80 million to the University of Chicago; supported Yale, Harvard, and Brown universities; and founded the Rockefeller Institute for Medical Research (now Rockefeller University) in New York.

Even more generous with his fortune was steel tycoon Andrew Carnegie (1835–1919). He strongly believed that a person who grows rich through the toil of society's laborers should share his wealth with those laborers through various social institutions. In his famous 1889 essay "The Gospel of Wealth," he stated:

> There remains, then, only one mode of using great fortunes. [It is a system in which] the surplus wealth of the few will become . . . the property of the many. . . . This wealth, passing through the hands of the few [into social institutions],

can be made a much more potent force for [good] than if it had been distributed in small sums to the people themselves.[27]

As in the familiar adage, Carnegie readily put his money where his mouth was. He established the Carnegie Institute for Scientific Research, funded more than two thousand public libraries, and gave $125 million in aid to colleges and other schools. By 1911, when he was seventy-six, he had given away fully 90 percent of his huge fortune. In this way, large portions of the wealth created by the Industrial Revolution were redistributed back into the ranks of society, bettering the lives of millions. Whether or not this ultimate outcome justifies the means by which said wealth was created in the first place, each individual must judge for him- or herself.

Chapter Three

THINKERS AND REFORMERS OF THE INDUSTRIAL AGE

The advent of the Industrial Revolution, first in Britain and later in the United States, France, and other nations, was widely recognized as a major historical turning point. For countless centuries people had made clothes, weapons, and other products by hand. Now machines were rapidly taking over manufacturing processes, changing the very nature of work and triggering major economic and social changes as well.

Philosophers, social critics, and social reformers were deeply interested in the wide-reaching changes they were witnessing. Most of those studying and discussing the changes were British and American thinkers; but there were also voices from France, Germany, and other countries that had steadily adopted industry in the nineteenth century.

These thoughtful individuals, who were influential in politics and society, saw certain benefits of industrialization. A larger variety of products could be made faster, for instance, they said. And these could be made available to more people at more affordable prices. This benefited individuals because the products usually made people's lives easier. The products also contributed to the country's economic growth, raising standards of living. Also, new inventions spawned by the Industrial Revolution were making communications and transportation quicker, which in turn expanded trade and made national economies grow.

At the same time, many of the thinkers and critics perceived a number of drawbacks and downsides in the rise of large-scale industry. These negative aspects of industrialization, they said, particularly affected those who toiled in the factories and in the mines that supplied industry with raw materials. A modern historian explains how some British and American social critics viewed the plight of the growing ranks of industrial workers:

> Excessively long hours, low pay, rigorous discipline, and subhuman working conditions were the most common grievances of early industrial workers. Many plants neglected hazards to their employees, few had safety devices to guard dangerous machinery, and cotton mills maintained [high] heat and [humidity]. Many workers could not afford decent housing, and if they could afford it, they could not always find it.[28]

Concerned thinkers and critics responded to these problems with a wide range of opinions and sometimes proposed solutions. Some, especially in the early stages of industrialization, felt that ills such as poverty and social inequality were natural and inevitable facets of large-scale industry and life in general. Others felt that these ills were not inevitable and that the economic system created by industrialization could be reformed. Some advocated that such reforms should be made from above, that

Classical economists Thomas Malthus (right) and David Ricardo (left) believed that poverty was an inevitable part of the industrial economy.

is, by the industrialists, upper classes, and laws enacted by governments. Others held that the changes should or were more likely to come from below, after protests, demands, strikes, or even violent revolutions by the workers.

Poverty and Inequality Inevitable?

Early thinkers who said that poverty among the workers was a natural, unavoidable part of the industrial economy were the so-called classical economists. The most famous classical economists were Britain's Thomas Malthus (1766–

1834) and David Ricardo (1772–1823). Both observed that the industrialization process tended to crowd poorer workers into urban slums. There, disease, insufficient supplies of food and clean water, and rampant crime reduced the quality of life. "A much greater proportion of poor people than in past ages," Malthus stated, are "employed in manufactures and crowded together in close and unwholesome rooms."[29] Increasing the workers' salaries, what he called the "price of labor," would not help them, he said. If factory owners raised wages, more poor farmers would move into the cities to acquire the better-paying jobs.

The "Iron Law of Wages"

Noted British economist David Ricardo explained his famous "iron law of wages" in the following manner:

It is when the market price of labor exceeds its natural price, that the condition of the laborer is flourishing and happy, that he has it in his power to command a greater proportion of the necessaries and enjoyments of life, and therefore to rear a healthy and numerous family. When, however, by the encouragement which high wages give to the increase of population, the number of laborers is increased, wages again fall to their natural price, and indeed from a re-

action sometimes fall below it. When the market price of labor is below its natural price, the condition of the laborers is most wretched. Then poverty deprives them of those comforts which custom renders absolute necessaries. It is only after their privations have reduced their number, or the demand for labor has increased, that the market price of labor will rise to its natural price, and that the laborer will have the moderate comforts which the natural rate of wages will afford.

David Ricardo, "On the Principles of Political Economy and Taxation," Library of Economics and Liberty. www.econlib.org/LIBRARY/Ricardo/ricP.html.

As a result, less food would be produced. Food prices would then rise, offsetting the wage increases and reducing all the workers once more to poverty.

Both Malthus and Ricardo also tied the plight of the poorer workers to natural increases in population. Ricardo, for example, formulated what came to be called the "iron law of wages." Essentially, it held that workers' wages would always tend toward a minimum level because of certain unchangeable natural forces. In this view, raising workers' pay would allow them to afford to have more children; in turn, that would produce more workers; and since more workers would be competing for the same jobs, many would be willing to work for less. That would cause wages to fall. And the cycle would repeat from one generation to another. It is perhaps not surprising that many factory owners used Ricardo's ideas to justify paying their employees low wages.

As time went on, however, several of the classical economists ideas were shown to be shortsighted. Neither Malthus nor Ricardo foresaw the enormous economic expansion that industry would bring to Britain and America, for instance. In many cases, there ended up being enough profits to make the bosses rich and pay fair wages to the workers at the same time. Also, the classical economists did not anticipate scientific advances that eventually allowed tremendous increases in food production, enough to feed vast numbers of workers at affordable prices.

Nevertheless, the notion that competition in an industrial society would inevitably make a few bosses wealthy at the expense of their exploited workers persisted. Even Andrew Carnegie, the industrialist who gave away most of his huge fortune, felt that this was the natural way of things. "Private Property, the [natural] Law of Accumulation of Wealth, and the [natural] Law of Competition [are] the highest result of human experience," he wrote.

[They are] the soil in which society so far has produced the best fruit. Unequally or unjustly, perhaps, as these laws sometimes operate [and cause inequalities in wealth and social status], and imperfect as they appear to the idealist, they are, nevertheless, like the highest type of man, the best and most valuable of all that humanity has yet accomplished.[30]

Indeed, Carnegie believed that paying workers high wages would be unproductive because most would spend the extra money on frivolous things. It was better for society, he thought, for men like himself to keep more of the money and give it to worthy social causes later.

Attempts at Reform from Above

In contrast, some thinkers held that the industry-driven economic system could be made fairer and more just by instituting reforms from above. They often proposed that society be reorganized to make industry and labor relations more equitable and to improve worker's lives. British liberal economist and philosopher John Stuart Mill (1806–1873), for example, advocated that such social reorganization should be accomplished mainly by companies and other private institutions and groups. He called for higher wages for workers and better education for them and other people of average means:

> An effective national education of the children of the laboring class, is the first thing needful: and, coincidently with this, a system of measures which shall . . . extinguish extreme poverty for one whole generation. . . . The aim of all intellectual training for the mass of the people, should be to cultivate common sense; to qualify them for forming a sound practical judgment of the [political and economic] circumstances by which they are surrounded.[31]

Mill also advocated allowing workers to form trade unions, a very unpopular idea at the time.

Mill felt that government should play as small a role as possible in private enterprise and people's lives. Yet he did see areas where national leaders and politicians could help make the economic system more just. In particular, he wanted to see them pass legislation to protect children who worked in factories and to give women workers, along with all women, the same political rights as men (another of his ideas that was ahead of its time).

Another advocate of reforming the system from above was wealthy British cotton mill owner Robert Owen (1772–1858). Well before Britain's government began enacting reforms, he voluntarily improved working and living conditions for his workers. In addition to reducing their hours and increasing their pay, he provided schooling for all children in the working families.

The results of these and other reforms were impressive. Owen rapidly transformed the village of New Lanark, Scotland, where his mills were located, into a model industrial town. Because the workers were treated humanely and with respect, they had little to complain about and productivity in the mills increased. So Owen benefited along with them. Eager to convince other industrialists to follow his lead, he released an essay to the public, posing the following question to fellow factory owners:

> Will you then continue to expend large sums of money to procure the best devised mechanism of wood, brass, or iron; to retain it in perfect repair . . . [but] not afford some of your attention to consider whether a portion of your time and capital would not be more advantageously [profitably] applied to improve your living machines [workers]?[32]

Proposed Reform from Below

Despite Owen's success, both as a businessman and reformer, for reasons that remain unclear few other industrialists

Young girls work in a factory during the Industrial Revolution in the 1870s.

followed his example. So improvements in the system directed from above were slow in coming. This provided fertile ground for those thinkers who argued that workers should push for reforming the inequalities of the machine age and industrial economy from below. Particularly critical of these ills was German philosopher Karl Marx (1818–1883). In his view, members of the working class (which he called proletarians) had become little more than machines themselves. They were increasingly exploited and forced into submission by their wealthy bosses (the bourgeoisie).

Another German thinker, Friedrich Engels (1820–1895), agreed with Marx. Together, in 1848 they published the *Communist Manifesto*, which described the rise of industrialism and the bourgeoisie this way:

> Steam and machinery revolutionised industrial production. The place of manufacture was taken by the giant, Modern Industry; the place of the industrial middle class by industrial millionaires, the leaders of the whole industrial armies, the modern bourgeois. Modern industry has established the world market, [which] has given an immense development to commerce. . . . As industry, commerce, navigation, [and] railways extended, [the] bourgeoisie developed, increased its capital [wealth], and pushed into the background every [other social] class.[33]

According to Marx and Engels, among the inequalities suffered by the working classes were long hours,

In Berlin, Germany, children sit in front of statues of German philosophers Karl Marx, left, and Friedrich Engels, whose 1848 publication The Communist Manifesto *discussed the risks of industrialism.*

Caring for One's "Living Machinery"

British industrialist and social reformer Robert Owen explained some of his progressive ideas to his fellow big business owners in his essay, "A New View of Society." (His term "living machinery" is a reference to his human workers.)

From experience which cannot deceive me, I venture to assure you, that your time and money so applied [put into reforms that favor the workers] would return you, not five, ten, or fifteen per cent for your capital so expended, but often fifty, and in many cases a hundred per cent. I have expended much time and capital upon improvements of the living machinery; and it will soon appear that time and the money so expended . . . are now producing a return exceeding fifty per cent. . . . [It makes good sense] to treat [one's worker] with kindness, that [his] mental movements might not experience too much irritating friction; to endeavor by every means to make [him] more perfect; to supply [him] regularly with a sufficient quantity of wholesome food and other necessaries of life, that the body might be preserved in good working condition, and prevented from being out of repair, or falling prematurely to decay.

Robert Owen, "A New View of Society," McMaster University. http://socserv2.socsci.mcmaster.ca/~econ/ugcm/3ll3/owen/newview.txt.

low pay, no pensions or other benefits, and mind-numbingly boring tasks:

Owing to the extensive use of machinery and to division of labor, the work of the proletarians has lost all individual character, and, consequently, all charm, for the workman. He becomes an appendage [added part] of the machine, and it is only the most simple, most monotonous, and most easily acquired knack, that is required of him. Hence, the cost of production of a workman is restricted, almost entirely, to the means of subsistence that he requires for his maintenance. . . . As the repulsiveness of the work increases, in the same proportion the burden of toil also increases, whether by [longer] hours, by increase of the work exacted in a given time, or by increased speed of the machinery.[34]

This inhuman treatment of workers could not go on indefinitely, Marx and Engels said. A struggle between society's haves and have-nots was inevitable, they claimed. The existing capitalist industrial economy was doomed and violent revolutions by the workers were inevitable. They would rise up, seize governmental power, and create a fairer, socialist system.

In socialism as these thinkers defined it, the government owns and operates society's means of production (the factories, mines, and so forth) for the people's greater good. Such large-scale socialist systems did not arise in Marx and Engels's lifetimes, however. This was partly because the existing industrial economy eventually expanded the middle classes in England, America, and elsewhere; so most workers felt little or no need to revolt. Violent socialist revolutions did occur in Russia and China in the twentieth century. But these produced repressive communist dictatorships that Marx and Engels, who advocated a fair, open government run by workers, would not have approved of.

Other Approaches to Economic Justice

Other thinkers wanted to see industrial society become more equitable but called for nonsocialist, nonviolent approaches to this goal. Among the more famous and influential among them was America's Henry George (1839–1897). Like Mill, Owen, and Marx, he saw that the rise of big industry had created a widening rift between society's haves and have-nots, including much poverty. "This association of poverty with progress is the great enigma [riddle] of our times," George said. "It is the central fact from which spring industrial, social, and political difficulties that perplex the world. . . . So long as all the increased wealth which modern progress brings goes but to build up [the] great fortunes [of the industrialists]. . . progress is not real and cannot be permanent. The reaction must come."[35]

By "reaction," George meant a drastic reordering of society, which might or might not be violent. He advocated the peaceful approach of reforming the tax system to make society more equitable for everyone. Basically, he called for eliminating private ownership of land. Instead, the government would own the land and people, including rich industrialists, would pay a rent-like tax for using it. No other taxes of any kind would exist. In theory, this would make society fairer because workers would retain enough money to make their lives comfortable. George's system was not socialism because in it the government would not own the factories. Rather, it would own only the land they occupy; therefore, the industrialists could still control their businesses and make as much money as they want.

The most extreme advocates of reforming industrialized society were the anarchists, who emerged in the early to mid-1800s. Among them were Frenchman Pierre-Joseph Proudhom (1809–1865) and American Benjamin R. Tucker (1854–1939). Contrary to popular opinion, they did not seek to destroy society. Instead, they sought to promote individual liberty and social justice by eliminating (or reducing to a bare minimum) most social institutions, including polit-

What Marx and Engels Did Not Foresee

The late, noted American historian Crane Brinton pointed out some of the economic and social forces that Marx and Engels did not foresee and that discouraged most of the social revolutions these thinkers predicted.

Marx oversimplified the complexities of human nature by trying to force it into the rigid mold of economic determinism [the idea that economic events, rather than political ones, shape history] and ignoring the nonmaterial motives and interests of [people]. Neither prole-tarians nor bourgeoisie have proved to be the simple economic stereotypes Marx supposed them to be. [Industry] has put its own house in better order and elimi-nated the worst injustices of the factory system. No more than Malthus did Marx [or Engels] foresee the notable rise in the standard of living that began in the mid-nineteenth century and has continued . . . down to our own day.

Crane Brinton et al., *A History of Civilization.* Englewood Cliffs, NJ: Prentice-Hall, 1995, p. 582.

ical parties, organized religion, police, and taxation. They held that when every worker became a free agent, he or she could either start a business or negotiate fair wages with an employer.

However, like Marxist socialism and other proposals for radical change, anar-chism did not catch on. By the late nine-teenth century, the Industrial Revolution had penetrated and transformed existing social classes and institutions. Put simply, most people compromised. They were willing to do their best to survive in the new, sometimes inequitable industrial sys-tem in exchange for the many modern products and conveniences it produced.

Chapter Four

INDUSTRY'S IMPACT ON THE ENVIRONMENT

Before the advent of the machine age, humans had made only a minimal impact on nature. Many large forests were still intact, and the wildlife they supported were still plentiful. The water in most streams was still clean. And air pollution was almost unheard of. The great Scottish-born American naturalist John Muir (1838–1914) described the preindustrial landscape of what is now the northeastern United States:

> [There] stretched dark, level-topped cypresses in knobby, tangled swamps, grassy savannas in the midst of them like lakes of light, groves of gay sparkling spice-trees, magnolias and palms, glossy-leaved and blooming and shining continually. [There also] rose hosts of . . . white pine and spruce, hemlock and cedar . . . their myriad [numerous] needles sparkling and shimmering, covering hills and swamps, rocky headlands and domes, ever bravely aspiring and seeking the sky. . . . Beaver meadows [existed] here and there, full of lilies and grass; lakes gleaming like eyes, and a silvery embroidery of rivers and creeks watering and brightening all the vast glad wilderness.[36]

After the coming of large-scale industry, however, such idyllic settings became more and more a part of the nostalgic past. At first in Britain, and later in America, smoke from industrial furnaces fouled the air. Wastes and chemicals were dumped into streams, lakes, and ocean inlets. Forests thinned and in some cases disappeared. And unsightly slag heaps (piles of mining wastes) marred once pristine mountainsides and meadows. Environmental destruction became so serious that a major conservationist movement eventually arose to combat it. Part of this effort took the form of government legislation intended to reduce or ban some of the worst pollution.

"Everything Around Is Blackened"

Because Britain was the first nation to industrialize on a large scale, industry's assault on the environment first became evident there. The environmental decline was at first small in scope. It was isolated to the immediate vicinity of the few initial and fairly small factory towns and to a handful of coal mines in the countryside. But as the Industrial Revolution accelerated in the late 1700s and early 1800s, the industrial towns rapidly expanded, in some cases covering many square miles. And the number of mines multiplied across the landscape.

One of the first and certainly the most visible of the undesirable environmental effects these industrial facilities created was air pollution. By the 1820s thousands of factories and mills belched soot-laden

Disdain for the "Snorting Steam"

English artist and writer William Morris (1834–1896) deeply regretted the environmental destruction that had swept across the English countryside in his lifetime. In his popular epic poem The Earthly Paradise *(published between 1868 and 1870), he envisioned a group of people searching for surviving remnants of a more ideal, purer world. The work begins with these references to the machine age and its polluting effects.*

Forget six counties overhung with smoke,
Forget the snorting steam and piston stroke,
Forget the spreading of the hideous town;
Think rather of the pack-horse on the down,

And dream of London, small, and white, and clean,
The clear Thames bordered by its gardens green;
Think, that below [the] bridge the green lapping waves
Smite some few keels that bear Levantine staves,
Cut from the yew wood on the burnt-up hill,
And pointed jars that Greek hands toiled to fill,
And treasured scanty spice from some far sea

William Morris, *The Earthly Paradise*, The Internet Sacred Text Archive. www.sacred-texts.com/neu/morris/ep1/ep103.htm.

A view of the river near Manchester, England. German writer Friedrich Engels wrote about the pollution of Manchester.

smoke into the atmosphere. A German traveler who visited the English factory town of Manchester was appalled. "There is no sun," he observed. "Here, there is always a dense cloud of smoke to cover the sun, while a light rain—which seldom lasts all day—turns the dust into a paste which makes it unnecessary to polish one's shoes."[37]

Air pollution so dense that it turns rain into a toxic brew seems incredible to most people today. Yet the phenomenon was widespread in many parts of Britain in the early to mid-1800s. In 1842 a government commission released a report, popularly known as *Report on Sanitary Conditions*, which stated, "The rainwater is frequently like ink."[38]

Natural water sources suffered no less from industrial pollution. Mills and factories were routinely built alongside rivers so that the moving water would provide power (by turning waterwheels and other means). For the sake of convenience, and with little or no regard for the environmental consequences, these facilities dumped their waste materials, including raw sewage, chemicals, and waste from new metallurgical processes, right into the water. In 1845, after a visit to England, German writer Friedrich Engels described the main river flowing through Manchester:

At the bottom flows, or rather stagnates . . . a narrow, coal-black, foul-smelling stream, full of debris and refuse, which it deposits on the shallower right bank. In dry weather, a long string of the most disgusting, blackish-green slime pools are left standing on this bank [and] give forth a stench unendurable even on the bridge forty or fifty feet above the surface of the stream. . . . Above the bridge are tanneries, [mills], and gasworks, from which all drains and refuse find their way into the [river].[39]

The cities were not the only areas affected. Noxious clouds of smoke and smog spread outward from the industrial towns and enveloped large swaths of rural England, Wales, and Scotland. Similarly, water that had been polluted in the cities flowed into the countryside. Meanwhile, most of Britain's few remaining forests were leveled, leaving an increasingly bleak landscape. In his 1848 novel *Dombey and Son*, the great English writer Charles Dickens described a typical section of blighted countryside:

Through the hollow, on the height [hill], by the orchard, by the park, by the garden . . . where the sheep are feeding . . . the mill is going [and] the factory is smoking. . . . Everything around is blackened. There are dark pools of water, muddy lanes, and miserable habitations far below. . . . Smoke and crowded gables, and distorted chimneys and deformity of brick and mortar penning up deformity of mind and body, choke the murky distance.[40]

Environmental Devastation in America

A similar assault on the environment took place in several areas of the United States. There, in fact, pollution of the landscape was an almost inevitable extension of a process that began in colonial times, even before the coming of large-scale industry. The Native Americans had for centuries used some of the continent's abundant natural resources, but they had left the environment intact and healthy. In contrast the Europeans who settled America in the 1600s and 1700s immediately began modifying the landscape to suit their particular needs and goals. As Muir puts it:

In the settlement and civilization of the country, bread more than timber or beauty was wanted. And in the blindness of hunger, the early settlers, claiming Heaven as their guide, regarded God's trees as only a larger kind of pernicious weeds. . . . Accordingly, with no eye to the future, these pious destroyers waged interminable [relentless] wars [on the forests and other aspects of the environment]. The smoke of their burning has been rising to heaven more than two hundred years.[41]

The rise of industry resulted in tens of thousands of miles of railroad track being laid, disturbing woods and forests. The smoke from the wood-burning engines created air pollution.

Burning forests turned out to be only one of many sources of the "smoke" Muir spoke of. Pollution and reshaping of land and waterways significantly increased as the Industrial Revolution spread in the United States. The problem was most evident at first in the environmental effects of the burgeoning textile industry, which began in New England.

Dams built to help harness water power for the factories reduced or wiped out several fish populations. People downstream who depended on fishing for their livelihoods or dinner tables suffered. Meanwhile, hazardous chemicals that the mills dumped into the rivers floated downstream. At the same time, rampant destruction of nearby forests caused large-scale soil erosion. Much of the excess soil ended up in the rivers, doing further damage.

As industry and economic prosperity spread, the country's population quickly expanded. Settlement moved westward from the eastern seaboard at a dizzying pace. And thousands of new farms and towns sprang up. This necessitated even more destruction of wooded areas; by 1850 some 37,000 square miles (96,000 sq. km) of forests were disappearing each year.

Industry also supplied transportation networks and vehicles to connect those farms and towns and move people and goods great distances. These included canals, steamboats, and the railroads with their smoke-belching locomotives and tens of thousands of miles of track. The locomotives were long powered by burning wood. At least a million cords of wood were used to power Ohio's railroads in 1885 alone. In that year and in the years that followed, the smoke from the trains combined with that from thousands of industrial smokestacks, which poured soot and chemicals into the air at an increasing rate in many parts of the country.

As in Britain, the environmental impact of the industrial age was not limited to American cities, industrial complexes, and mines. As the railroads expanded westward and brought hordes of new settlers, many animal species were hunted to near or total extinction. Natural populations of wolves, mountain lions, coyotes, and bears, which threatened domestic livestock, were devastated. The giant herds of bison (or buffalo) that had roamed the prairies for millions of years suffered the same fate. Once numbering as many as 75 million, only a few hundred of them were left by the mid-1880s.

Still another unexpected environmental impact of American industrialization was widespread devastation of soil in the Midwest and West. In addition to cutting down forests, farmers in these regions applied new industrial inventions to agriculture, including tractors and mechanized harvesters. These allowed farmers to open up millions of new acres to cultivation. But in many cases they also exposed soil that was too arid to farm effectively. Such careless mechanized farming practices (combined with prolonged drought) eventually led to disaster. In the infamous dust bowl of the 1930s, huge tracts of soil (covering an estimated 100 million acres, or 40 million ha) became useless for farming. The dry, dusty soil fed immense dust storms. More than half a million residents of the affected regions were driven to flee to other states.

Moving Toward Solutions

In both Britain and the United States, attempts to reduce such environmental damage were at first slow in coming. One of the earliest concrete attempts to address the problem occurred in 1834. A London manufacturing company had for some time been releasing industrial wastes into the Thames River. City officials eventually brought charges against the owners, who were found guilty. Part of the indictment read:

> Defendants unlawfully and injuriously conveyed great quantities of

The conservationist movement began in earnest when President Theodore Roosevelt set aside large pieces of land for protection from industrial development.

Dickens Describes Coketown

In Charles Dickens's novel Hard Times, *published in 1854, the setting is a fictional city called Coketown. It was based in large part on the real town of Preston (in west-central England), as well as on the many similar English industrial cities that had become crowded and polluted.*

Coketown lay shrouded in a haze of its own, which appeared impervious to the sun's rays. You only knew the town was there, because you knew there could have been no such sulky blotch upon the prospect without a town. A blur of soot and smoke, now confusedly tending this way, now that way, now aspiring to the vault of Heaven, now murkily creeping along the earth, as the wind rose and fell, or changed its quarter: a dense formless jumble, with sheets of cross light in it, that showed nothing but masses of darkness. Coketown in the distance was suggestive of itself, though not a brick of it could be seen.

Charles Dickens, *Hard Times*, Book 2, Chapter 1, Project Gutenberg. www.gutenberg.org/dirs/etext97/hardt10.txt.

Hard Times *by Charles Dickens was based on English industrial cities.*

filthy, noxious, unwholesome . . . liquids, matters, scum and refuse into the river Thames, whereby the waters became charged and impregnated with the said liquid and became corrupted and unfit for the use of his Majesty's subjects. . . . People who supported themselves and their families by catching and selling fish were deprived of their employment and reduced to great poverty and distress, all to the common nuisance and grievous injury of his Majesty's subjects, to the evil example, and against the peace.[42]

Such successful actions against industrial polluters were rare, however, until the twentieth century. It was only then that major efforts were made to improve Britain's and America's environments. A large portion of those efforts were guided by the modern conservationist movement. A few scattered individuals had called for reversing the damage to the environment and conserving rather than destroying natural resources in the mid- to late 1800s. But no significant progress was made until President Theodore Roosevelt (served 1901–1909) set aside large sections of wilderness for protection from industrial exploitation. Thereafter, the U.S. Congress, as well as the British Parliament, steadily passed laws regulating various industries in an effort to reduce environmental damage. It should be emphasized, however, that these developments were not motivated solely out of love and concern for nature.

Rather, more selfish economic worries and precautions played larger roles, as historian William Beinart explains:

The mission [of forestry conservation] was increasingly the commercial propagation [creation] of trees. The rationale behind conservationism . . . was [mainly] concern over the continuing health of the national economy—even the future of American civilization and great nation status itself. . . . British forest management, in similar fashion, was governed by the fact that Britain imported more than 90 percent of its timber in the early twentieth century [and therefore needed to replenish some of its forests].[43]

As the twentieth century progressed and public worries about the ravages of industrial pollution increased, legislators in both countries responded by passing pro-environment bills. The U.S. Oil Pollution Act of 1924, for example, banned the intentional dumping of petroleum products and wastes into coastal waters. And the so-called Clean Air Acts enacted in Britain in 1956 and America in 1963 were the first of a series of laws designed to fight air pollution caused primarily by industry. A major step forward was the creation of the U.S. Environmental Protection Agency in 1970. Its main functions are to regulate and enforce the environmental laws passed by Congress.

Thus, a number of steps have been taken in the past century to reduce the

Industrialization and Global Warming

Mounting evidence shows that a large portion of climate change, or global warming, has been caused by accumulated air pollution generated by the Industrial Revolution since the early 1800s. In August 2007 the Associated Press reported the following fact, based on a study released that same month by the prestigious journal Science.

A round the middle of the 19th century, the Arctic took a sooty turn for the worse, according to researchers studying how humans have affected the climate.

Soot can darken the snow, causing it to absorb sunlight, warm up and melt. That, in turn, can add to local climate warming by exposing darker ground which absorbs energy from the sun that the white snow would have reflected.

Ice cores from before about 1850 show most soot came from forest fires. But since then, soot in the snow has increased several times over and most now comes from industrial activities, according to a paper in the online edition of the journal *Science*.

In a separate paper in that journal, a team of British researchers forecast that climate warming will slow for about a decade, then bound back to record-setting temperatures.

Randolph E. Schmid, Associated Press. "Humans Leave Sooty Footprint in Arctic Ice." *USA Today*, August 9, 2007. http://www.usatoday.com/tech/science/environment/2007-08-09-climate-change-arctic-soot_N.htm.

environmental damage caused by large-scale industrialization. However, industrial polluters still exist in many parts of the world, especially in nations that have only recently begun to industrialize, like India and China. Moreover, considerable evidence exists that gases released into the atmosphere since the Industrial Revolution began have significantly contributed to the present climate change crisis, often referred to as global warming. Thus, issues relating to industry's effects on the environment are likely to persist well into the foreseeable future.

Chapter Five

HEALTH AND MEDICAL INNOVATIONS

One of the more pressing social issues surrounding the Industrial Revolution was the health of those who toiled in the factories, mines, and other industrial centers. Expert observers began speaking of "occupational hazards." They also coined terms such as "occupational health" to describe the relationship between one's job and one's health. There seemed to be a connection between occupational health risks and adverse environmental conditions created by a number of industries. Over time, it became clear that at least some industrial workplaces, processes, and materials had harmful effects on workers' health.

Some examples of unhealthy and dangerous work conditions were obvious even in the earliest years of industrialization. In particular, coal miners and others who toiled underground day in and day out clearly had more health

problems and shorter lives than most other workers. Eventually, some miners wrote pamphlets to try to educate the public about their plight. One such tract said that a miner

> often labors from ten to fifteen hours mid-thigh deep in water. The pernicious exhalations [filthy air] from which entail upon him . . . chronic diseases, and in some instances deprive him of sight, while the total absence of one breath of air fit for respiration never fail to wear out, in a few years, the hardiest constitution [physical condition]. In a few years he becomes exhausted from excessive labor [and unhealthy working conditions].[44]

It is important to emphasize that some aspects of human health actually

improved during the Industrial Revolution. Indeed, the industrial age witnessed a host of medical advances, including the realization that germs cause disease. The fact is that the machine age spurred more than economic growth; it also encouraged and made possible numerous scientific discoveries and advances, including medical ones. As historian Bert Hansen puts it, "Medicine became recognizably 'modern' in the nineteenth century, producing new inventions, new theories, new curative powers, [and] gradually replacing the trial-and-error inventiveness that had long characterized medical practice."[45]

Overcrowding Leads to Health Problems

At first, however, the medical problems caused by industry were much more obvious than the medical improvements brought by the machine age. Overcrowding in industrial towns and cities repeatedly led to unsanitary conditions. In turn these increased the incidence of illness and disease. For a long time the poor workers who dwelled in these areas could do little or nothing to remedy the situation. This is because they lacked the political voice and economic clout needed to

John Ruskin Denounces Industry

John Ruskin was a noted artist, art critic, Oxford professor, and romantic who detested the Industrial Revolution. In an 1870 pamphlet addressed to English workers, he said that modern industrial towns were so filthy and unsanitary that they bred disease. One powerfully worded passage read:

The horrible nests, which you call towns are little more than laboratories for the distillation into heaven of venomous smokes and smells, mixed with effluvia [gaseous wastes] from decaying animal matter, and infectious miasmata [vapors] from purulent [pus-causing] disease. . . . [Society should] absolutely forbid noxious [toxic] manufactures [industries]; and [should instead be] planting in all soils the trees which cleanse and invigorate earth and atmosphere. [At present, every river is] a common sewer, so that you cannot so much as baptize an English baby but with filth, unless you hold its face out in the rain, and even that falls dirty.

Quoted in J.M.W. Turner, R.A., "Ruskin, the Industrial Revolution, and the Greenhouse Effect." www.jmwturner.org/ruskin_page.htm.

make society aware of their plight and to push lawmakers to enact needed reforms.

Therefore, it fell on concerned prominent individuals in the middle and upper classes to point out the increasing health problems associated with large-scale industrialization. Many of these people were physicians. On the front lines in humanity's ongoing war against disease and illness, they saw firsthand the relationships between sickness and the conditions in which people lived.

A pioneer in this area was British doctor Thomas Southwood Smith (1788–1861). In 1830 he published his groundbreaking book, *A Treatise on Fever*. In addition to listing the symptoms of various fever-producing illnesses, Smith made a direct connection between disease epidemics and the impoverished, unsanitary living conditions of the industrial workers. The causes of malaria, typhoid fever, and other "fevers," he said, might well lie in people's "modes of life [lifestyles], in the habits of society, in the structures of houses, in the condition of public streets, and the common sewers."[46] Medical science did not yet know that germs cause disease. But Smith had correctly pinpointed the unsanitary conditions in which it would later be shown that disease germs thrive and multiply. His book inspired a number of medical, social, and environmental reformers in both Britain and the United States.

Doctors in another rapidly industrializing nation, Germany, also pointed out some of the occupational health problems suffered by industrial workers. In 1845 a German social reformer interviewed several physicians who had such workers as patients. One doctor reported:

The very frequent incidence of anemia [abnormally low levels of red blood cells] among girls employed in factories deserves special mention. The hard work, the crowding of many individuals into closed rooms [in the factories, where they get too little] exercise in the fresh air . . . are sufficient explanation of this disease. The same condition also exists among the needlewomen, dressmakers, etc.[47]

Another doctor described serious health problems among the residents of industrial slums, especially children:

The dwellings of the working classes mostly face the yards and courts. The small quantity of fresh air admitted by the surrounding buildings is [negated] by the [fumes] from stables and [garbage heaps]. These dwellings are therefore always filled with fetid [rotten] air and steam, which condenses on the walls and creates green mold. The adults escape the worst influences by leaving [for work] during the day, but the children are exposed to it with its full force.[48]

Reform Efforts

In these same years, physicians, social critics, and others began to call for reforming working and living conditions in industrial towns in order to improve public health. In 1832, for instance, British doctor Charles T. Thackrah (1795–1833) released the first important work addressing the issue of occupational health. Its title was *The Effects of the Principle Arts, Trades and Professions, and of Civic States and Habits of Living, on Health and Longevity*. Thackrah not only agreed with Smith about the link between adverse industrial conditions

A nineteenth-century illustration shows overcrowding in a London slum during the Industrial Revolution.

The "Evils" in the Mills

Charles T. Thackrah's 1832 book called for improvements and reforms of working conditions in various professions, including many in factories and other industrial settings. In this passage, he points out some of the problems he discovered while inspecting British cloth-making mills, in which workers operated large power looms.

The principal evil we find in the mills is the closeness of the atmosphere. The [workrooms], though large . . . are generally crowded with looms, and by no means sufficiently ventilated. . . . The weaving produces no dust, but there is an [odor that] certainly [affects] the purity of the atmosphere. Several of the workers suffer from head-ache and disorders of the stomach. . . . Silk weavers are affected with pain in the region of the stomach, from leaning against the beam, and with disorder of the digestive organs, from the bad quality or defective quantities of their food.

Charles T. Thackrah, *The Effects of the Principle Arts, Trades and Professions, and of Civic States and Habits of Living, on Health and Longevity.* London: Longman Rees, 1832, pp. 36–38.

and health, he also made several suggestions for reversing some of the ill effects of the Industrial Revolution. Employment in many forms of industry, Thackrah stated, can be

in a considerable degree injurious to health. [Some people think] that the evils cannot be counteracted, and urge that an investigation of such evils can produce only pain and discontent. From a reference to fact and observations I reply that in many of our occupations the injurious agents might be immediately removed or diminished. Evils are suffered [allowed] to exist, even when the means of correction are known and easily applied. Thoughtlessness or apathy is the only obstacle to success. . . . When moreover, an evil is kept before the public attention . . . the advance of science [can] often provide a remedy.[49]

In the years that followed, Thomas Southwood Smith also began actively working to improve public health by reforming the industrial system. He followed up his earlier *A Treatise on Fever* by establishing the Health of Towns Association, which studied the issues of public health and made recommendations for improvements. In the 1840s and 1850s, Smith also traveled to America. There, he advised and helped like-minded reformers who were working to improve health conditions in U.S. factories and other workplaces.

Equally, if not more, important and influential on both sides of the Atlantic was the 1842 *Report on Sanitary Conditions*, spearheaded by noted British public official Edwin Chadwick. The report was particularly critical of overcrowding in workers' housing in the industrial towns.

Combined with pollution dumped in those towns by the factories, the report stated, such overcrowding had seriously increased the incidence of disease:

Disease caused, or aggravated, or propagated chiefly amongst the [industrial] laboring classes by atmospheric impurities produced by decomposing animal and vegetable substances, by damp and filth, and

Public health became a concern during the Industrial Revolution and several individuals worked on reforming both living and working conditions in industrial towns. Edwin Chadwick (pictured) worked on the Report on Sanitary Conditions.

close and overcrowded dwellings prevail amongst the population in every part of the kingdom. . . . Such disease, wherever its attacks are frequent, is always found in connection with the physical circumstances above specified, and that where those circumstances are removed by drainage, proper cleansing, better ventilation, and other means of diminishing atmospheric impurity, the frequency and intensity of such disease is abated; and where the removal of the noxious agencies appears to be complete, such disease almost entirely disappears.[50]

Dangerous Industrial Products

Reformers noted that bad working and living conditions were not the only threats posed to public health by industry. There were also poisons in various manufactured goods that were causing serious health problems. One of the worst was lead, then a common ingredient in paints and other products. Over time it became increasingly clear that exposure to lead could cause brain damage. Among the leading reformers in this area was Britain's Thomas M. Legge (1863–1932). He wrote several books about lead-paint poisoning and other industrial illnesses. He also joined with American, French, German, and other reformers in calling for bans on using lead paint inside factories, homes, and other structures.

Although the public at large was vulnerable to lead and other dangerous substances created by industry, the workers who directly made and regularly handled these substances were even more at risk. Research began to show that prolonged exposure to various kinds of industrial products could cause specific diseases. In fact, one modern occupational health organization states, many of these ailments

first gained public attention during the Industrial Revolution in the 19th century. . . . Examples include silicosis, a lung disease of miners, industrial workers, and potters exposed to silica dust; scrotal skin cancer in chimney sweeps exposed to soot; neurological disease in potters exposed to lead glazes; and bone disease in workers exposed to phosphorus in the manufacture of matches. . . . Industrial society has introduced or increased human exposure to thousands of chemicals in the environment. Examples are inorganic materials such as lead, mercury, arsenic, cadmium, and asbestos, and organic substances such as polychlorinated biphenyls (PCBs), vinyl chloride, and the pesticide DDT. Of particular concern is the delayed potential for these chemicals to produce cancer.[51]

Concerns over workers' exposure to such chemicals inspired Britain's Parliament to pass the Factories and Workshops Act in 1867. This important legislation imposed regulations on the manufacture and handling of dangerous substances in industries such as match making, paper staining, and explosives production.

The bill also improved occupational health by prohibiting some individuals from working in certain industries. Children younger than twelve and women could not work in a mill in which glass melting took place, for example. This was because the glassmaking industry was particularly dangerous. Furnaces and large quantities of molten glass often caused serious burns. Sometimes the molten glass would explode because of gases trapped in it, which also caused serious injuries. And no child younger than eleven could be employed at grinding metal, which was also an especially dangerous job. Other similar acts targeting occupational illnesses were passed in Britain in the years that followed. Among them were bills in 1878 and 1883 that banned children from factories that made lead paints.

Crucial Medical Breakthroughs

Meanwhile, there was another side of the coin, so to speak, of health and medicine in the Industrial Revolution. At the same time that factories, mines, and the slums surrounding them caused many health problems, the machine age encouraged new scientific research into improving human health. People were inspired by the innovative spirit of the age to apply human know-how to all sorts of problems, including health and wellness. This brought about numerous breakthroughs in knowledge and technology in many areas, including biology and medicine. From the

Ether is used for the first time during surgery in Boston, Massachusetts, in 1846. The use of ether as an anesthetic dulled the patient's pain and resulted in a medical breakthrough.

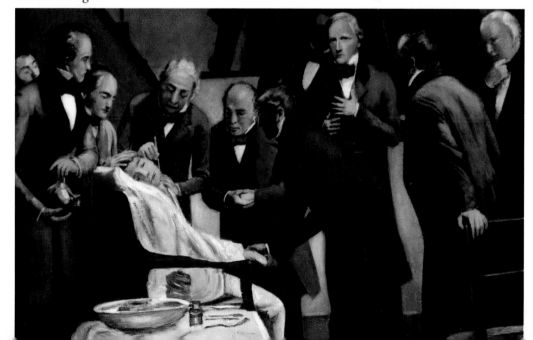

Lister's Antiseptic Experiments

One of the great heroes of science and society during the Industrial Revolution was a British surgeon named Joseph Lister (1827–1912). During the years that Pasteur and other researchers were trying to prove that germs cause disease, Lister did not wait for that proof. If germs did kill people, Lister decided, he must act immediately to avoid needless deaths. So he applied some simple sanitary techniques in his work at a hospital in Glasgow, Scotland. In 1864 he started washing various kinds of wounds with carbolic acid. The results were dramatic. After one year the death rate from infections developing from such wounds fell from 50 to 10 percent. Lister went on to make strict rules about sterilizing hands, linens, and medical instruments to kill any germs that might be on them. Lister's antiseptic (germ-fighting) experiments not only saved many lives, including those of thousands who worked in British factories, they also lent strong support to the germ theory that Pasteur and others were trying to get the medical community to accept.

British surgeon Joseph Lister sprays carbolic acid onto a patient during one of his earliest antiseptic surgical operations, circa 1865. His sanitary techniques dramatically reduced the number of infections from wounds.

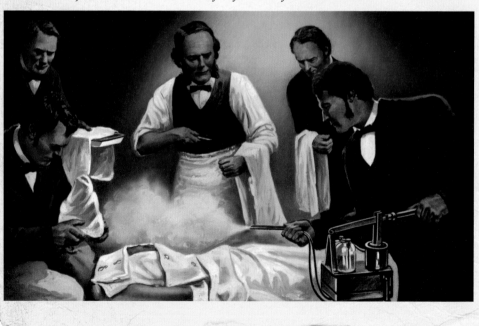

late 1800s on, the medical advances rapidly began to alleviate human suffering.

One of the first of these medical breakthroughs was the discovery of effective anesthetics (substances that dull pain during surgery). The earliest anesthetic was ether. It was first used successfully in an operation at Massachusetts General Hospital in Boston in 1846. Before that time, Hansen explains:

> most surgery simply could not be undertaken. Even if physicians proved willing to inflict horrible pain, a patient writhing from it could not be held still enough for the surgeon's scalpel to do its delicate work. Surgery had thus been limited to a few types of procedures, [including removal] of superficial growths on the skin, and amputation of a badly damaged limb. . . . The ability to banish pain during surgery . . . was a medical breakthrough of the highest order.[52]

Even more groundbreaking was the realization that germs cause disease. Scientists had known about the existence of germs since the late 1600s. But they had assumed that these tiny creatures had no harmful effects on people. In the 1850s French scientist Louis Pasteur (1822–1895) showed that certain kinds of germs cause wine to spoil. This made him suspect that other kinds of germs might cause disease. In the next three decades, he and a few other brilliant researchers, including German physician Robert Koch (1843–1910), confirmed that this was indeed the case.

After that, modern medicine rapidly progressed, producing one exciting breakthrough after another. In 1885 Pasteur developed a vaccine to treat rabies. Soon afterward other researchers introduced treatments for tuberculosis, diphtheria, and typhoid fever, diseases that together had killed tens of thousands of people each year. Another crucial breakthrough was the introduction of X-ray technology, allowing doctors to see inside the body. These and other medical advances "had a profound effect on people's thinking," Hansen writes. They "reversed the assumption that older doctors and older medicines were better than new ones. [They also] created a new expectation that medicine can and should change, that progress is to be expected, that the new advances would come from laboratory experiments."[53]

This expectation that progress would better people's lives, and was therefore good, had long been a guiding force of the industrial age. Certainly, the Industrial Revolution had made more products available to more people. And it had made a few industrialists and nations rich and prosperous. But it was through advances in medicine and public health that modern science and technology first radically transformed the lives of millions of industrial workers for the better.

Chapter Six

Artistic and Literary Reactions

The Industrial Revolution in Britain, the United States, and elsewhere brought about a radical transformation of society at every level. Writers and artists of every stripe could not help but be profoundly moved, influenced, and motivated by it all. Some waxed eloquent about what they saw as the upward march of progress. Others found success by selling their works to wealthy individuals and, like them, indulged in the excesses of the Gilded Age. Still others were disturbed by such excesses and denounced them. Meanwhile, novels, nonfiction books, essays, poems, paintings, songs, and eventually photos and films captured the lives of both the rich and poor in industrial society.

Some of the creators of these works became leading social critics. They roundly condemned the substandard working and living conditions of those who toiled in the factories and mines, as well as the environmental destruction caused by industry. They also exposed corruption and dangerous practices in various industries, educating the public and helping to inspire reform. Often such critical assaults were delivered in the guise of fiction, especially in the most popular literary form of the age—the novel. Among the more famous examples are Charles Dickens's novels *Dombey and Son* and *Hard Times*. Despite some imaginary towns and characters, these works contain accurate, vivid descriptions of nineteenth-century industrial working and living conditions. A similar case was American writer Upton Sinclair's novel *The Jungle*. It described unsanitary practices in the meatpacking industry so realistically that legislators soon passed new laws regulating that industry.

British Literary Responses

The earliest literary responses to the Industrial Revolution were shorter and less specific. Mostly poems and essays, they were written in Britain, where modern industry first arose in the 1700s. The most memorable of these writings today are those of what scholars call the British romantics, who lived and worked in the late eighteenth and early nineteenth centuries. Prominent among them were William Wordsworth, Samuel Taylor Coleridge, and William Blake. They mostly looked to the past, to the supposed "good old days," for inspiration and comfort, and they disapproved of the rapid industrial, urban, and population growth occurring around them. Wordsworth (1770–1850), for example, was particularly unhappy about the effects of large-scale industry on nature. In his view, the urban sprawl spurred by large-scale industrialization was swallowing up the once wide and pristine countryside. This theme stands out in his 1814 poem, "The Excursion":

> Here a huge [industrial] town, continuous and compact
> Hiding the face of earth for leagues, and there,
> Where not a habitation [house or village] stood before,
> Abodes of men . . . spread through spacious tracts.
> O'er which the smoke of unremitting fires [from furnaces]
> Hangs permanent, and plentiful as wreaths
> Of vapor glittering in the morning sun.
> And, wheresoever the traveler turns his steps
> He sees the barren wilderness erased,
> Or disappearing.[54]

A younger contemporary of Wordsworth, the influential Scottish historian and essayist Thomas Carlyle (1795–1881), was more analytical. As a historian, he sought to understand and define the onrush of industry and to place it in historical context with prior ages. In his essay "Signs of the Times: The Mechanical Age" (1829), he described how machines and the social, economic, and political customs associated with them were steadily altering people's lives. In the process, traditional work methods, thinking, and morality were rapidly disappearing. "It is the Age of Machinery," he stated.

> [It is] the age which, with its whole undivided might, forwards, teaches and practices the great art of adapting means to ends. Nothing is now done directly, or by hand; all is by rule and calculated contrivance [plan]. Our old modes of exertion [work methods] are all discredited, and thrown aside. On every hand, the living artisan is driven from his workshop, to make room for a speedier, inanimate one [a machine]. The shuttle drops from the fingers of the weaver, and falls into iron fingers that ply it faster. . . .

There is no end to machinery. [Indeed] we have an artist that hatches chickens by steam; the very brood-hen is to be superseded [replaced]! For all earthly, and for some unearthly purposes, we have machines.[55]

Carlyle did not overtly condemn the ongoing process of industrialization. Machines were practical, he admitted, and allowed humans to manipulate nature as never before: "We remove mountains, and make seas our smooth highway; nothing can resist us. We war with rude Nature; and, by our resistless engines, come off always victorious, and loaded with spoils." Yet he also warned of the danger of losing a certain level of social and moral stability that had existed in preindustrial times: "By our skill in [building machines] it has come to pass that in the management of external things we excel all other ages; while in whatever respects the pure moral nature, in true dignity of soul and character, we are perhaps inferior to most civilized ages."[56]

British writers also used the novel to enlighten and educate readers about potential abuses of industrial workers. In addition to Dickens's renowned efforts

Rydal Mount, a house once occupied by British poet William Wordsworth, in the countryside of Cumbria, England. Wordsworth disapproved of and wrote about the ill effects of industrial growth on nature.

Wordsworth on the "Darker" Side of Industry

British poet William Wordsworth was highly critical of many aspects of the Industrial Revolution. In this passage from his poem "The Excursion," he first concedes that the machine age has made Britain economically prosperous. But at what price? he seems to ask as he points out that industry has also caused much damage to the environment.

Hence is the wide sea peopled, hence the shores

Of Britain are resorted to by ships
Freighted from every climate of the world

With the world's choicest produce. Hence that sum

Of keels that rest within her crowded ports

Or ride at anchor in her sounds and bays;

That animating spectacle of sails

That, through her inland regions, to and fro

Pass with the respirations of the tide,
Perpetual, multitudinous! . . .

I grieve, when on the darker side

Of this great change I look; and there behold

Such outrage done to nature as compels

The indignant power to justify herself;

Yea, to avenge her violated rights.

For England's bane.

William Wordsworth, "The Excursion," Internet Modern History Sourcebook. www.fordham.edu/halsall/mod/1814wordsworth.html.

in this genre, an outstanding example was *Mary Barton: A Tale of Manchester Life*, by Elizabeth Gaskell (1810–1865). Published in 1848, it realistically described the difficult, poverty-stricken lives of the factory workers in Manchester, one of Britain's leading industrial cities. In one passage, after a fire ravages a mill owned by the wealthy Carson family, many workers lose their meager but essential incomes. A pall of depression then descends over the slums surrounding the factory:

There were homes over which Carsons' fire threw a deep, terrible gloom; the homes of those who would fain [like to] work, [and] the homes of those to whom leisure was a curse. There, the family music was hungry wails, when week after week passed by, and there was no work to be had, and consequently no wages to pay for the bread the children cried aloud for in their young impatience of suffering. There was no breakfast to lounge over; their lounge was taken in bed, to try and keep warmth in them in that bitter March weather, and, by being quiet, to deaden the gnawing wolf [of hunger] within.[57]

American Writers and the Factory System

Similar literary reactions to the social and economic effects of industrialization were penned in the United States. There, the textile business was the first to industrialize on a large scale. So most early American writings about the factory system depicted cotton and other textile mills. The first American novel to do so was *The Factory Girl*, written in 1814 by Sarah Savage. The story follows the experiences of an orphaned girl who makes a comfortable life for herself by working in a Massachusetts mill. Like a number of early American descriptions of developing industry, the book took a largely positive view of its effects.

But as time went on and the ill effects of industrialization became more obvious, writers became more critical. Some saw machines and factories as cold and dehumanizing. An important example was the 1826 short novel *The Man Machine*, by James K. Paulding (1778–1860, a New York writer who also served as U.S. navy secretary). An example of social satire (spoof) and dark humor, the work features a factory owner who openly admits that he sees his workers as flesh-and-blood versions of his power looms and other machines. In a lecture to them, he says: "I consider the people employed in my establishment as part of the machinery. [It is] my duty and interest to combine [them, so] that every hand, as well as every spring, lever, and wheel, shall [effectively] cooperate to produce the greatest [gain] to [me], which [is what I call] the Man Machine."[58]

By the 1840s American writers were also warning about the moral dangers for young women working in textile mills. As women crossed old social barriers and went to work in factories, some people were especially troubled by the prospect of industrial bosses taking advantage of their female employees sexually. In the 1844 novel *The Belle of Lowell*, by Ellen Merton, a factory owner seduces some of his workers. He also forces them into prostitution.

Some writers proposed ways to counteract such perceived evils of industrial society. Often in these fictional accounts, religion saved the workers, and by extension society itself, from harm. Boston-born Elizabeth S. Phelps (1844–1911) wrote a popular children's book, *Up Hill, or Life in the Factory*, in 1865. It depicts two laborers who overcome their harsh working conditions and poverty by accepting the teachings of Christianity. Phelps also wrote a popular 1871 adult novel, *The Silent Partner*, in which the main character is an idealistic social reformer. A woman who inherits a textile mill, she devotes her life to making working conditions better for her employees.

Depictions of Steamboats and Railroads

American writers and artists also vividly captured the images and early eras of two of the machine age's pivotal forms of transport—the steamboat and the railroad. The majority of these observers celebrated, rather than criticized, what were called the "steamer" and "iron horse." A major example is the nostalgic, almost loving, way that noted chronicler of Americana Mark Twain (1835–1910) depicted the steamers on the Mississippi River in the nineteenth century. As a young man, Twain had been a steamboat pilot. So it is not surprising that steamers and the people who rode in

them appear prominently in three of his most famous novels—*The Adventures of Tom Sawyer* (1876), *Life on the Mississippi* (1883), and *The Adventures of Huckleberry Finn* (1884). *Life on the Mississippi* contains detailed descriptions of a voyage down the Mississippi on a large, elegantly decorated steamboat, a sort of "floating palace."

Romantic visions of steamboats and the culture that surrounded them also appear frequently in the art of the period.

Artists and writers, most prominently Mark Twain, frequently used steamboats as subjects in their work. Shown here is Steamboat Race on the Mississippi *by George F. Fuller.*

Twain's Romantic Memory of Steamboats

In his Life on the Mississippi *(1883), Mark Twain made the point that the old steamboats were like "floating palaces." His was a romantic, largely positive literary view of one of the main symbols of the early decades of the Industrial Revolution.*

When he stepped aboard a big fine steamboat, he entered a new and marvelous world. Chimney-tops cut to counterfeit a spraying crown of plumes— and maybe painted red; pilot-house, hurricane deck, boiler-deck guards, all garnished with white wooden filigree work of fanciful patterns; gilt acorns topping the derricks; gilt deer-horns over the big bell; gaudy symbolical picture on the paddle-box, possibly; big roomy boiler-deck, painted blue, and furnished with Windsor armchairs. Inside, a far-receding snow-white "cabin;" porcelain knob and oil-picture on every stateroom door; curving patterns of filigree-work touched up with gilding, stretching overhead all down the converging vista; big chandeliers every little way, each an April shower of glittering glass-drops; lovely rainbow-light falling everywhere from the colored glazing of the skylights; the whole a long-drawn, resplendent tunnel, a bewildering and soul-satisfying spectacle! . . . Every state-room had its couple of cozy clean bunks, and perhaps a looking-glass and a snug closet.

Mark Twain, *Life on the Mississippi*, Chapter 38, Project Gutenberg. www.gutenberg.org/files/245/245-h/p8.htm#c38.

In his novel Life on the Mississippi, *Mark Twain referred to old steamboats as "floating palaces."*

Famous for its engravings and prints, the nineteenth-century company Currier and Ives put out many detailed prints of steamboats. They were shown moving downriver, engaging in races, and suffering fires and other disasters. These were among the company's most popular products in all parts of the country. Similarly, many painters chose the steamer as a subject. Among them were widely admired marine artists James Bard (1815–1897) and his brother John Bard (1815–1856). They created thousands of handsome portraits of steamboats that for later generations became popular keepsakes from a bygone era.

Popular culture also developed around the nineteenth-century American railroads, which were the subject of works of literature, prints, paintings, music, and films. Many of the literary works dealing with the railroads described their impact on the American West. Among the more famous are *The Gilded Age* (1873) by Mark Twain and *The Octopus* (1901) by novelist Frank Norris (1870–1902). Norris's work depicts struggles, some of them bloody, between wealthy railroad companies and small farmers in then mostly rural southern California. Although the author's sympathies clearly lie with the underdogs—the farmers—he accepts that the railroads are part of progress and necessary.

Throughout the West and elsewhere, the rise of the railroads also spawned numerous popular songs. Some of these, including "I've Been Working on the Railroad" and "She'll Be Coming 'Round the Mountain," remain American classics. Another classic, "John Henry," describes a legendary African American railroad worker who dies while competing against a steam-driven machine. The lyrics of an early version include:

John Henry was hammering on the right side, the big steam drill on the left. Before that steam drill could beat him down, he hammered his fool self to death. . . . John Henry was lying on his death bed. He turned over on his side, and these were the last words John Henry said: "Bring me a cool drink of water before I die."[59]

The often romantic mystique of the railroads inspired early moviemakers as well. Among the first widely popular silent films was *The Great Train Robbery*, directed by Edwin S. Porter and released in 1903. It contained some of the first movie action scenes ever, among them the robbery and a person being thrown from a moving train.

Exposing Corruption and Injustice

Sharply contrasting with the popularized romance of steamboats and railroads were literary depictions designed to expose and hopefully reform darker aspects of large-scale industry. A number of big American businesses were riddled with corruption and/or regularly cheated their customers. One of the worst offenders in this area was the food industry, in particular meatpacking factories that employed unsanitary methods.

These practices were exposed by novelist Upton Sinclair (1878–1968) in one of the most widely read and important books ever written by an American. *The Jungle*, published in 1906, features a fictional meat packer, Jurgis Rudkis, an

The Jungle, *by Upton Sinclair, exposed corruption and unsanitary practices in the meatpacking industry.*

Horrors of the Dust Bowl

The great American writer John Steinbeck effectively captured the environmental catastrophe of the Dust Bowl in these lines from his classic novel, The Grapes of Wrath.

The dawn came, but no day. In the gray sky a red sun appeared, a dim red circle that gave a little light, like dusk; and as that day advanced, the dusk slipped back toward darkness, and the wind cried and whimpered over the fallen corn. Men and women huddled in their houses, and they tied handkerchiefs over their noses when they went out, and wore goggles to protect their eyes. When the night came again it was black night, for the stars could not pierce the dust to get down. . . . The people, lying in their beds, heard the wind stop. They awakened when the rushing wind was gone. They lay quietly and listened deep into the stillness. . . . In the morning the dust hung like fog, and the sun was as red as ripe new blood. All day the dust sifted down from the sky, and the next day it sifted down. An even blanket covered the earth. It settled on the corn, piled up on the tops of the fence posts, piled up on the wires; it settled on roofs, blanketed the weeds and trees.

John Steinbeck, *The Grapes of Wrath,* Internet Archive. www.archive.org/stream/grapesofwrath030650mbp/ grapesofwrath 030650mbp_djvu.txt.

immigrant from Lithuania. However, the horrendous abuses Rudkis witnesses in the course of his job were very real when Sinclair described them. He told how meat packers routinely treated rotten meat with chemicals to make it look fresh, then packaged it in cans for grocery store shelves. The following passage from the book details another grotesque practice: "There was a trap in the pipe [in the filthy floor of the meat-canning room], where all the scraps of meat and odds and ends of refuse were caught, and every few days it was the old man's task to clean these out and shovel their con-

tents into one of the trucks with the rest of the meat [bound for market]!"[60]

Not surprisingly, the corruption exposed in Sinclair's book provoked public outrage. Only months after the book's release, Congress passed the Pure Food and Drug Act and the Meat Inspection Act, which imposed needed regulations on many sectors of the food industry.

In the years that followed, popular novels also exposed various examples of suffering and injustice that had been more indirectly caused by big industry. One major example was the plight of the thousands of poor farmers forced to flee the ravages of the Dust Bowl (caused partly by the mechanization of agriculture) in the Midwest in the 1930s. This story was beautifully told in John Steinbeck's powerful novel *The Grapes of Wrath* (1939). Many years had passed since the British romantics had complained about the spoilage of nature by encroaching machine-based society. Yet Steinbeck's word pictures of the devastated Midwest were hauntingly similar. In some ways, literary responses to the grimmer aspects of the industrial age had truly come full circle.

Chapter Seven

EFFECTS ON GLOBAL SOCIETY

The Industrial Revolution developed to its greatest extent first in Britain and then in the United States. Consequently, most modern studies of the industrial age dwell mainly on how it affected the societies of those two pivotal nations. However, the Industrial Revolution also had a number of effects on global society, as well.

When the factory system and other aspects of industrialization spread from Britain, they took root at first in other European countries or lands that had been heavily settled by Europeans. Thus, for a long time the Industrial Revolution was almost strictly a European or Western phenomenon. (Japan, in eastern Asia, was the only exception initially.) The early acquisition of major industrial capacity gave that handful of mostly Western nations a huge amount of power and influence. Indeed, they swiftly achieved global dominance. Jeff Horn, a leading scholar of the Industrial Revolution, elaborates:

Europeans and their descendants living in North America, South Africa, Australia, New Zealand, Algeria, and many other places scattered around the world became the masters of the planet. The Industrial Revolution facilitated the development of Western military superiority and the new, improved means of transportation tied the globe together in a far more concrete manner, allowing the exploitation of vast new areas. At minimal cost, Europeans and their descendants came to enjoy an unprecedented degree of world domination as a result of the Industrial Revolution.[61]

"The Sun Never Sets on the British Empire"

Not surprisingly, the first country to industrialize on a large scale—Britain—was also the first to use its newfound power to exploit and dominate less-developed societies around the world. The captains of British industry required a continuous supply of raw materials, many of which were scarce or nonexistent in Britain. Also, to turn a handsome profit, they needed as many markets as possible in which to sell their manufactured goods.

With these needs in mind, the British created the first true global empire. By the late 1700s, Britain had established colonies overseas, particularly in North America. But the thirteen American colonies had broken away in the 1770s and in the 1780s and formed the United States. This was a considerable loss to British society. However, Britain more than made up for it in the years that fol-

Britain's large-scale industrialization allowed it to dominate less-developed societies around the world.

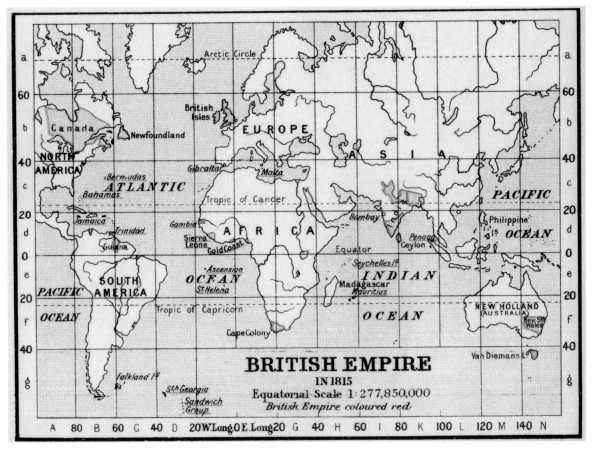

lowed by gaining control over numerous nonindustrialized areas of the globe. In most cases, factories and other major aspects of industry remained in Britain. And the exploited lands became the suppliers of raw materials and labor.

Moreover, this new and larger British Empire was more of an economic and social entity than a territorial one. In other words, it exploited the markets and dominated the societies of many foreign lands without ruling them directly. Often local leaders were in charge. But they and their societies remained heavily dependent on Britain's industrial economy and the trade it generated far and wide.

Thus, economic relationships were central to Britain's expanding empire. To sustain these foreign connections and markets, the British often drew up treaties, which of course were worded in ways that best served their own interests. But they were willing to use force if negotiation did not work. Thanks in part to more effective and lethal weapons turned out by British and American industry (especially in the second half of the nineteenth century), Britain was able to intimidate a number of world leaders and populations who opposed its economic domination. That domination became especially pronounced in South Africa, India, China, Egypt, Singapore, and Australia. It is no wonder, therefore, that the phrase "the sun never sets on the British Empire" was coined in this era, in which Britain's Industrial Revolution reached its height.

The way this process worked is clearly illustrated by British-controlled India, which in the 1800s became the most valuable colony in the world. Horn explains how Britain expanded its industrial base and achieved added economic prosperity at the Indians' expense:

[First] India became a key market for British manufactured goods. In 1854, India absorbed 13 percent of British trade.... By 1900, the volume of [this trade] had tripled. [British] exports to India were almost exclusively cotton textiles and the products of the iron and metal industries.... To prevent competition with [British-based industries], the British intentionally [kept] India [from becoming industrialized] beginning in the late [1700s]. As India's own industries were throttled . . . India became an enormous importer of British textiles. [This] vast trade . . . ensured the profitability of British mills and forced the poor peasants of India to find other means of paying their taxes and making a living.[62]

New Industrial Powers

Britain was unable to maintain its near monopoly on large-scale industry and global economic domination indefinitely, however. Other leading political and economic Western powers were not far behind. Besides the United States, which developed a major textile industry in the early 1800s, prominent among the early giants was France. There, certain circumstances delayed major industrial development for several decades. First, France had far less coal at its disposal than Britain did, and coal was the chief source of power during the early years of the industrial age. Also, during the late 1700s and early 1800s, while Britain was rapidly industrializing, the French were caught up in social and political turmoil. The chaotic French Revolution and destructive Napoleonic Wars absorbed most of France's creative energies and money in this period.

Once France seriously applied itself to industrialization, however, it steadily began to close the gap with Britain. The French experienced impressive industrial and economic growth between 1815 and 1870, in part because they built a railroad network comparable to Britain's.

Like the British, the French saw that they could become more economically prosperous by collecting the natural resources of and finding new markets in nonindustrial societies, when possible their own colonies. Two-time French prime minister Jules Ferry explained the importance of this approach in 1890. "Colonial policy is the daughter of industrial policy," he said.

For rich nations, where capital [money] is abundant and accumulates rapidly, where manufactures consistently increase, exportation [of industrial products] is an essential factor in public prosperity. . . . Today, the whole world wants to spin and weave, to forge and distill [and] social peace is, in the indus-

trial age of humanity, a question of markets. . . . The European market is saturated. [So] it is necessary to discover new groups of consumers in other parts of the world.[63]

In this way France exploited foreign colonies and markets, especially in Indochina (the Asian region now made up of Vietnam, Laos, Cambodia, and Thailand). The swiftly industrializing Belgians did the same in the Congo, in central Africa. There, in the 1880s and 1890s, they extracted the raw materials that fueled an enormous rubber industry. (In the process, they horribly brutalized the natives, killing millions through forced labor and neglect.) Meanwhile, the Dutch made substantial economic inroads into South Africa. And the Germans, too, scrambled to industrialize on a big scale. As one modern observer points out:

The German government wanted to hasten the process and catch up with British industrialization. Germany used its rich iron and coal resources to develop heavy industry, such as iron and steel manufacture. It also proved to be an environment that encouraged big businesses and cooperation among large firms. The German banking sector, for example, was dominated by a few large banks that coordinated efforts to increase industry.[64]

Raw materials for German industry and the labor to extract them came not

Other countries began to industrialize on a large scale in order to catch up with Britain, including Germany, with its emphasis on iron and steel.

Industry a Civilizing Influence?

Although the majority of nineteenth-century Europeans had no moral reservations about exploiting foreign peoples, a few did. For example, French economist Paul Beaulieu, quoted here, felt that his country, and others with factory systems and the great wealth these systems produced, should export many of the advantages of industrial society to colonized regions. Beaulieu saw the peoples of these regions as racially or otherwise inferior, as most Europeans of that era did. But he felt a duty to reduce that inferiority by "civilizing" the natives.

A great part of the world is inhabited by [inferior peoples], knowing so little of the arts and being so little accus- tomed to work and invention that they do not know how to exploit their land and its natural riches. . . . [The industrialized nations must provide] the inhabitants [of these regions] with some education and regular justice, teaching them the division of labor and the uses of capital [money] when they are ignorant of these things. It opens an area not only to the merchandise of the mother country, but to its capital and its savings, to its engineers, its overseers, [and] to its emigrants [those who move to the colony].

Quoted in Mount Holyoke College, "Leroy-Beaulieu on the Desirability of Imperialism, 1891." www.mtholyoke .edu/acad/intrel/beaulieu.htm.

only from Germany itself, but also from its colonies in Africa. The Germans controlled an estimated 9 percent of Africa by 1914.

Latecomers to the Machine Age

During the late 1800s and early 1900s, some regions of Europe and North America lagged behind their more industrialized neighbors. Russia was a prime example. Though large and populous, it retained a largely agricultural economy long after Britain, France, the United States, and others had developed major industrial bases. In part, this was because of the Russian institution of serfdom. More than 20 million people, comprising a third of the nation's population, were serfs, slave-like laborers who toiled on the estates of wealthy landowners. As long as Russia's chief menial workers were tied by long-standing tradition to the land, the government, headed by emperors called czars, could not realistically enact a major changeover to an industrial economy. For decades, therefore, the Russians relied primarily on manufactured goods imported from Britain, Germany, and other leading Western industrial nations.

However, Russia was finally able to make a more substantial entry into the Industrial Revolution in the last few decades of the nineteenth century. This was possible partly because the serfs were finally freed, as Laura Frader explains:

The emancipation of the Russian serfs in 1861 meant that large numbers of rural folk were now free to work in large cities. [Also] massive railway building in the 1870s allowed Russia to exploit its immense natural resources of coal and iron more effectively than ever before, and factories began to appear in cities such as Moscow and St. Petersburg.[65]

Other regions lagged behind in industrial development. Spain was one. Southern Italy and the American South also retained primarily agricultural economies well after their immediate neighbors had

Even after the serfs were freed and Russia began adopting industry, large numbers of Russians remained poor agricultural workers, including those shown in this 1917 photo. One-third of Russia's population had once been serfs.

built up industrial bases. Meanwhile, in Asia the transition from agriculture to industry proceeded at an even slower rate overall. China, Korea, Taiwan, India, and other Asian regions did not begin industrializing until well into the twentieth century. In large part, this was because they had long been exploited and purposely kept in a backward technological state by major Western industrial powers like Britain and France.

In contrast, the one major exception in Asia, Japan, launched a modernization program that brought it roughly into parity with the major Western nations. That program, known as the Meiji Restoration, began in 1868 and lasted about forty years. Realizing that, like the rest of Asia, they lagged far behind the industrialized West, Japanese leaders launched a crash industrialization program. It included constructing a railroad system; paving many formerly dirt roads and eventually acquiring automobiles to modernize transportation; installing extensive telegraph and later telephone lines; and building hundreds of modern-style factories, shipyards, and mines. At

Japan Industrializes

Japan's rapid industrial transformation in the late 1800s astounded many observers in the West, who had assumed that Asians were incapable of such ingenuity and effective organization. Two modern scholars summarize Japan's impressive transformation:

Japan's reorganization [included the creation of] a Western-style army and navy. . . . New banks were established to fund trade and provide investment capital [for industry]. Railways and steam vessels improved national communications. Many old restrictions on commerce, such as guilds and internal tariffs, were removed. Land reform cleared the way for individual ownership and stimulated production. Government initiative dominated manufacturing because of lack of capital and unfamiliar technology. A ministry of industry was created in 1870 to establish overall economic policy and operate certain industries. Model factories were created to provide industrial experience, and an expanded education system offered technical training [for factory managers and workers]. Private enterprise was involved in the growing economy, especially in textiles. . . . By the 1890s, huge industrial combines [corporations] had been formed. Thus, by 1900, Japan was fully engaged in an industrial revolution.

Michael Adas and Marc J. Gilbert, "Russia and Japan: Industrialization Outside the West," *World Civilizations*, AP Edition Companion Web site. http://wps.ablongman.com/long_stearns_wcap_4/18/4652/1190942.cw/index.html.

first the government built the factories, then sold them to well-to-do business-people at low prices. The goal here was to create a class of enterprising industrialists where none had existed before.

These massive reforms of the country's society and economy paid off for Japan. By 1920 almost a quarter of its social and economic energies were devoted to manufacturing and mining. Moreover, a hefty portion of this national industrial output was devoted to weapons and war production. This allowed the nation's increasingly militaristic leaders to launch aggressive wars against Russia, China, and eventually the United States.

A Smaller World

As Japan, Russia, and other nations became industrialized, they built navies of steam-driven ships like those the British, Americans, and French already possessed. Vast fleets of merchant vessels increasingly circled the globe. And in a sense, the early twentieth century dawned on what seemed to many people to be a much smaller world than had existed in the past.

Moreover, these and other aspects of large-scale industrialization proved irresistible. Almost as if the onrush of technology had a life of its own, the Industrial Revolution reached ever outward, transforming region after region and people after people. In Frader's words:

Even parts of the world that did not industrialize were touched by the power of new inventions, machines, and manufacturing processes, and by the products that the wheels of industry churned out. For the captains of industry produced goods in order to sell, trade, or barter [them], and their commercial activities circled the globe.[66]

For a long time, this outward reach of the elite industrialized nations was mostly one-sided. And it decidedly favored them and their own interests. Poorer, nonindustrialized countries and societies—what are today called the third world—were consistently exploited and drained of their material and human resources. The industrialized countries searched out "labor forces that were less organized, less militant, less powerful, and posed less of a physical threat to them," Horn points out. "Europeans and their descendants had always treated other groups as inferior, [and] native populations were pushed aside [or exploited] all over the world to make way for European enterprise."[67] Industrialized Japan displayed the same superior attitude and exploitative practices in dealing with China and its other less-developed neighbors.

When necessary, the industrialized few imposed their will on the nonindustrialized many by force. Here, too, industry had supplied the tools. In addition to merchant ships, steam had been applied to warships, which the big powers sent in large numbers around the globe. Steam-driven warships allowed

The Benefits of Colonies

In the late nineteenth century, leaders of the major industrial powers readily recognized the benefit of having overseas colonies from which to draw raw materials for various industries at home. In a speech delivered in 1885, Otto von Bismarck, chancellor of Germany, described some of the more valuable foreign regions to exploit:

I think that the most promising colonies are those of New Guinea. . . . According to my information, there are large and easily cultivable territories [that are] suitable for the cultivation of coffee, cotton, and similar tropical products. Colonies like Cuba, like Puerto Rico, like the West Indies, and the equatorial colonies [especially in Africa] are always given a high monetary value by their mother country. The main thing is to set up plantations there and to employ Germans with the highest or an advanced education [as overseers] on those plantations.

Quoted in Sidney Pollard and Colin Holmes, eds., *Documents of European Economic History: The Process of Industrialization, 1750–1870.* New York: St. Martin's, 1968, pp. 172–73.

Britons raise their flag after England takes over the eastern portion of New Guinea; Germany held the northern portion. Both countries benefited from colonization during the Industrial Revolution.

the British to extend their power and influence along the broad rivers of Africa and Asia. From the 1860s on, these war machines became increasingly sheathed in metal and carried cannons that unleashed explosive shells of enormous destructive power. Native populations lacking industries of their own could not stand up to repeating rifles, machine guns, and eventually mechanized tanks and airplanes that rained death and destruction from above.

This global imperative of the strong exploiting the weak could not be sustained indefinitely, however. Societies lacking industrial capacity increasingly sought to enjoy their own pieces, however small, of the worldwide economic pie. And these desires finally began to find expression at the end of World War II. Colonialism (the age-old system of imperial powers exploiting colonies) now became an unaccepted policy. The United Nations (UN) was created in 1945 and promoted the concept that all countries should have equal respect and opportunities. One of the organization's most important and influential statements in this regard was:

> The subjection of peoples to alien [outside] subjugation, domination, and exploitation constitutes a denial of fundamental human rights, is contrary to the Charter of the United Nations, and is an impediment to the promotion of world peace and co-operation. All peoples have the right to self-determination; by virtue of that right they freely determine their political status and freely pursue their economic, social and cultural development.[68]

Such statements did not instantly end the practice of strong, developed nations unfairly dominating weak, undeveloped ones. But global society was changing in ways that would make this more and more a thing of the past. In the last years of the twentieth century, China and India began emerging as industrial giants. And by the start of the twenty-first century, most countries had instituted some sort of industrialization, even if on a small scale. The global effects of this process over the course of the next century are difficult to predict. But it may well be that the still ongoing Industrial Revolution, which once divided the world into haves and have-nots, may ultimately prove a force for international shared interests, equality, and cooperation.

Notes

Introduction: On the Verge of a Great Movement

1. Laura L. Frader, *The Industrial Revolution: A History in Documents*. New York: Oxford University Press, 2006, p. 12.
2. Quoted in A.G. Keller and M.R. Davie, eds., *Essays of William Graham Sumner*. New Haven, CT: Yale University Press, 1940, pp. 92–93.
3. Matthew Josephson, *The Robber Barons*. New York: Harcourt, 1962, p. v.
4. Henry George, *Progress and Poverty*. New York: Appleton, 1883, p. 20.
5. John Burroughs, *The Summit of the Years*. Boston: Houghton Mifflin, 1913, p. 67.
6. Quoted in Keller and Davie, *Essays of William Graham Sumner*, p. 93.

Chapter One: Resistance to a Changing World

7. Frader, *The Industrial Revolution*, p. 114.
8. James L. Outman and Elizabeth Outman, *Industrial Revolution: Primary Sources*. Detroit: Gale, Cengage Learning, 2003, p. 55.
9. Kirkpatrick Sale, *Rebels Against the Future: The Luddites and Their War on the Industrial Revolution*. Cambridge, MA: Perseus, 1996, p. 5.
10. Quoted in Outman and Outman, *Industrial Revolution*, pp. 57–58.
11. Outman and Outman, *Industrial Revolution*, p. 64.
12. Quoted in J.L. Hammond and Barbara Hammond, *The Town Laborer, 1760–1832*. London: Longmans, Green, 1917, p. 173.
13. Quoted in G.D.H. Cole and A.W. Filson, eds., *British Working Class Movements: Selected Documents*. London: Macmillan, 1967, pp. 114–15.
14. Quoted in Frank Peel, *The Risings of the Luddites, Chartists, and Plug-Drawers*. London: Frank Cass, 1968, pp. 47–48.
15. Quoted in Sale, *Rebels Against the Future*, pp. 111–12.
16. Quoted in Max Beer, *A History of British Socialism*. London: Routledge, 2002, pp. 138–39.
17. Quoted in History Matters, "The Lowell Mill Girls Go on Strike, 1836." http://historymatters.gmu.edu/d/5714.
18. Frader, *The Industrial Revolution*, p. 114.
19. Quoted in Cole and Filson, *British Working Class Movements*, pp. 207–9.

Chapter Two: The "Robber Barons" and the Gilded Age

20. Maury Klein, "The Robber Barons' Bum Rap," *City Journal*, Winter 1995.

www.city-journal.org/html/5_1_a2.html.

21. Klein, "The Robber Barons' Bum Rap."

22. Quoted in Howard Zinn, *A People's History of the United States*. New York: HarperCollins, 2005, p. 261.

23. Quoted in Silas Hubbard, *John D. Rockefeller and His Career*. Self-published, 1904, p. 46.

24. Zinn, *A People's History of the United States*, pp. 251–52.

25. Quoted in Lowell National Historical Park, "The Boardinghouse System." www.nps.gov/archive/lowe/loweweb/Lowell_History/boardinghouse.htm.

26. MSN Encarta, "History of United States Business." http://encarta.msn.com/encyclopedia_701610399_2/History_of_United_States_Business.html.

27. Andrew Carnegie, "Carnegie, Gospel of Wealth," Swarthmore College. www.swarthmore.edu/SocSci/rbannis1/AIH19th/Carnegie.html.

Chapter Three: Thinkers and Reformers of the Industrial Age

28. Crane Brinton et al., *A History of Civilization*. Englewood Cliffs, NJ: Prentice-Hall, 1995, p. 571.

29. Thomas Malthus, "An Essay on the Principle of Population as It Affects the Future Improvement of Society," Rogers State University. www.faculty.rsu.edu/~felwell/Theorists/Malthus/Essay.htm#99.

30. Carnegie, "Carnegie, Gospel of Wealth."

31. John Stuart Mill, *Principles of Political Economy*, Book 2, Chapter 13, Library of Economics and Liberty. www.econlib.org/library/Mill/mlP.html.

32. Robert Owen, "A New View of Society," McMaster University. http://socserv2.socsci.mcmaster.ca/~econ/ugcm/3ll3/owen/newview.txt.

33. Karl Marx and Friedrich Engels, *The Communist Manifesto*, Chapter 1, Marxists Internet Archive. www.marxists.org/archive/marx/works/1848/communist-manifesto/ch01.htm.

34. Marx and Engels, *The Communist Manifesto*.

35. George, *Progress and Poverty*, p. 12.

Chapter Four: Industry's Impact on the Environment

36. John Muir, "American Forests," Electronic Text Center, University of Virginia Library. http://etext.virginia.edu/etcbin/toccer-new2?id=MuiAmer.sgm&images=images/modeng&data=/texts/english/modeng/parsed&tag=public&part=all.

37. Quoted in W.O. Henderson, *Industrial Britain Under the Regency*. London: Frank Cass, 1968, pp. 34–35.

38. Quoted in Sales, *Rebels Against the Future*, p. 57.

39. Friedrich Engels, *The Condition of the Working Classes in England*. Moscow: Progress, 1973, p. 79.

40. Charles Dickens, *Dombey and Son*. London: Tauchnitz, 1848, p. 200.

41. Muir, "American Forests."

42. Quoted in Professor K, Radford University, "Environmental History Timeline." www.runet.edu/~wkovarik/envhist/4industrial.html.

43. William Beinart, *Environment and History*. London: Routledge, 1995, pp. 45–46.

Chapter Five: Health and Medical Innovations

44. Quoted in Frader, *The Industrial Revolution*, p. 120.

45. Bert Hansen, "Medical Practices in Nineteenth-Century America," *History Now*, December 2006. www.historynow.org/12_2006/historian6.html.

46. Thomas Southwood Smith, *A Treatise on Fever*. London: Longman, Rees, 1830, p. 368.

47. Quoted in Sidney Pollard and Colin Holmes, eds., *Documents of European Economic History: The Process of Industrialization, 1750–1870*. New York: St. Martin's, 1968, pp. 497–500.

48. Quoted in Pollard and Holmes, *Documents of European Economic History*, pp. 497–500.

49. Charles T. Thackrah, *The Effects of the Principle Arts, Trades and Professions, and of Civic States and Habits of Living, on Health and Longevity*. London: Longman, Rees, 1832, pp. 7–8.

50. Quoted in The Victorian Web, "Chadwick's Report on Sanitary Conditions." www.victorianweb.org/history/chadwick2.html.

51. Robert C. Byrd Center for Rural Health, "Environmental and Occupational Diseases Overview." http://crh.marshall.edu/envirohealth/overview.htm.

52. Hansen, "Medical Practices in Nineteenth-Century America."

53. Hansen, "Medical Practices in Nineteenth-Century America."

Chapter Six: Artistic and Literary Reactions

54. William Wordsworth, "The Excursion," Internet Modern History Sourcebook. www.fordham.edu/halsall/mod/1814wordsworth.html.

55. Thomas Carlyle, "Signs of the Times: The Mechanical Age," Internet Modern History Sourcebook. www.fordham.edu/halsall/mod/carlyle-times .html.

56. Carlyle, "Signs of the Times."

57. Elizabeth Gaskell, *Mary Barton: A Tale of Manchester Life*, Project Gutenberg. www.gutenberg.org/dirs/etext00/mbrtn11.txt.

58. James K. Paulding, *The Man Machine*. Whitefish, MT: Kessinger, 2004, pp. 12–13.

59. Quoted in Ibiblio.org, "John Henry: Steel-Driving Man." www.ibiblio.org/john_henry/early.html.

60. Upton Sinclair, *The Jungle*, Chapter 5, The Literature Network. www.online-literature.com/upton_sinclair/jungle/5.

Chapter Seven: Effects on Global Society

61. Jeff Horn, *The Industrial Revolution*. Westport, CT: Greenwood, 2007, p. 119.

62. Horn, *The Industrial Revolution*, p. 123.
63. Quoted in Pollard and Holmes, *Documents of European Economic History*, pp. 169–70.
64. Quoted in MSN Encarta, "The Industrial Revolution Around the World." http://encarta.msn.com/encyclopedia_761577952_5/Industrial_Revolution.html.
65. Frader, *The Industrial Revolution*, p. 99.
66. Frader, *The Industrial Revolution*, p. 97.
67. Horn, *The Industrial Revolution*, p. 132.
68. United Nations, "Declaration on the Granting of Independence to Colonial Countries and Peoples." www.unhchr.ch/html/menu3/b/c_coloni.htm.

Time Line

1765
The introduction of the spinning jenny begins to revolutionize the textile industry in Britain.

1775
Scotsman James Watt introduces an efficient steam engine.

1786
Cloth makers in Leeds, England, sign a petition to protest their substandard working conditions.

1789
The French Revolution begins.

1810
In South America, Argentina gains its independence.

1812
In England the Luddites, workers opposed to industrialization, attack factories.

1815
French dictator Napoléon Bonaparte is defeated at Waterloo.

1824
Female textile workers in Pawtucket, Rhode Island, go on strike to protest a pay cut.

1836
Samuel F.B. Morse invents the telegraph, an enormous advance in communications.

1842
Britain's government sponsors the *Report on Sanitary Conditions*, which details environmental problems caused by industry.

1848
Socialist writers Karl Marx and Friedrich Engels publish their *Communist Manifesto*; English novelist Charles Dickens publishes *Dombey and Son*, which describes industrial towns.

1859
English naturalist Charles Darwin publishes *The Origin of Species*.

1861–1865
The Union and the Confederacy fight the American Civil War.

1881
U.S. president James Garfield is assassinated.

1883
American philosopher Henry George, a

critic of industrialism, publishes his book *Progress and Poverty*.

1885
French scientist Louis Pasteur develops a vaccine for rabies.

1906
American novelist Upton Sinclair publishes *The Jungle*, which is sharply critical of the meatpacking industry.

1911
By this year noted American industrialist Andrew Carnegie has given away 90 percent of his vast fortune.

For More Information

Books

T.S. Ashton and Pat Hudson, *The Industrial Revolution, 1760–1830.* New York: Oxford University Press, 1998. An excellent general look at the early years of the Industrial Revolution. Hudson, an economic historian, provides commentary updating Ashton's classic 1949 book.

William Dudley, ed., *The Industrial Revolution: Opposing Viewpoints.* San Diego: Greenhaven, 1998. A collection of articles about the effects of the Industrial Revolution.

Laura L. Frader, *The Industrial Revolution: A History in Documents.* New York: Oxford University Press, 2006. One of the best collections of primary sources for the Industrial Revolution.

Maury Klein, *The Change Makers.* New York: Times Books, 2003. Contains well-crafted profiles of Andrew Carnegie, John D. Rockefeller, and other major captains of American industry who helped to shape the industrial and technological revolutions.

Carolyn Merchant, *The Columbia Guide to American Environmental History.* New York: Columbia University Press, 2002. A useful overview of environmental history and issues, including the impact of the Industrial Revolution on the environment.

Charles Moore, *Understanding the Industrial Revolution.* London: Routledge, 2000. A clearly written volume that makes the Industrial Revolution accessible to nonscholars.

Patrick O'Brien and Roland Quinault, eds., *The Industrial Revolution and British Society.* Cambridge: Cambridge University Press, 1993. A well-written account of how the Industrial Revolution affected society.

Kirkpatrick Sale, *Rebels Against the Future: The Luddites and Their War on the Industrial Revolution.* Cambridge, MA: Perseus, 1996. This eye-opening volume examines the extreme negative reactions of some people in Britain to ongoing industrialization.

Upton Sinclair, *The Jungle.* New York: Doubleday, 1906. Sinclair's uncompromising exposé of the meatpacking industry in the late nineteenth century remains important and at times riveting reading. Many later reprints are available.

Peter N. Stearns, *The Industrial Revolution in World History.* Boulder, CO: Westview, 2007. A straightforward look at the Industrial Revolution and how it changed the world.

Alan Trachtenberg, *The Incorporation of America: Culture and Society in the Gilded Age.* New York: Hill and Wang, 2007. A well-written, insightful exploration of how the rise of major industry affected people's attitudes, lifestyles, and cultural pursuits.

Susan Zlotnick, *Women, Writing, and the Industrial Revolution*. Baltimore: Johns Hopkins University Press, 2001. An original and valuable study of women workers and writers and their contributions to the Industrial Revolution.

Internet Sources

Bert Hansen, "Medical Advances in Nineteenth-Century America," *History Now*, December 2006. www.historynow.org/ 12_2006/historian6.html.

Maury Klein, "The Robber Barons' Bum Rap," *City Journal*, Winter 1995. www.city-journal.org/html/5_1_a2 .html.

Steven Kreis, "Karl Marx, 1818–1883," The History Guide: Lectures on Modern European Intellectual History. www.historyguide.org/intellect/marx.html.

Web Sites

The Industrial Revolution, Internet Modern History Source Book (www.fordham.edu/halsall/mod/modsbook14.html). A very useful collection of articles on the Industrial Revolution, including several on its social, political, and urban effects.

The Industrial Revolution: An Overview, The Victorian Web (www.victorianweb.org/technology/ir/irov.html). A very helpful compilation of short articles on Industrial Revolution topics, including textiles, railroads, inventors, engineers, a chronology, and much more.

The Richest Man in the World: Andrew Carnegie, PBS (www.pbs.org/wgbh/amex/carnegie). PBS's excellent online site about one of the major captains of American industry in the nineteenth and early twentieth centuries.

Index

as unavoidable, 36–37
Progress and Poverty (George),
  10
Protests
  in textile industry, 19–21
  by wool mill workers, 16–19,
    20
Proudhom, Pierre-Joseph, 42
Pure Food and Drug Act (1906),
  77

R
Railroads, *49*
  depictions of, 72
  pollution from, 50
  songs inspired by, 75
Report on Sanitary Conditions, 47,
  61–62
Ricardo, David, *35,* 36, 37
Robber barons, 23
  See also Industrialists
The Robber Barons (Josephson),
  10
Robinson, Harriet H., 20–21
Rockefeller, John D., 10, 25, *26*
  philanthropy of, 30, 33
Roosevelt, Theodore, *51,* 53
Ruskin, John, 58
Russia, 84–85
Rydal Mount, *68–69*

S
Sale, Kirkpatrick, 16
Savage, Sarah, 71

*Signs of the Times: The Mechanical
  Age* (Carlyle), 67–68
The Silent Partner (Phelps), 71
Sinclair, Upton, 66, 75
Smith, Thomas Southwood, 58,
  60–61
Socialism, 42
Steamboat Race on the Mississippi
  (Fuller), *73*
Steamboats, 72–74
Steinbeck, John, 77, 78
Strikes
  in Britain, 19
  employers' responses to, 21,
    27–28
  in U.S. textile industry, 20
Sumner, William Graham, 8–9, 12,
  13, 27

T
Textile industry
  in Britain, 15–16
  environmental damage from,
    50
  in U.S., 20, 27–28, 71
Thackrah, Charles T., 59–60
Trade unions, 38
  employers' response to, 21
A Treatise on Fever (Smith), 58, 60
Tucker, Benjamin R., 42
Twain, Mark, 72–73, 75

U
United Nations, 89

Picture Credits

About the Author

In addition to his acclaimed volumes on the ancient world, historian Don Nardo has written and edited many books for young adults about modern European and American history, including *The Age of Colonialism, The French Revolution, The Atlantic Slave Trade, The Declaration of Independence, The Great Depression,* and *World War II in the Pacific.* Nardo also writes screenplays and teleplays and composes music. He lives with his wife, Christine, in Massachusetts.